T0355056

ORGANIZATIONAL STORYTELLING:

A LEADERSHIP CONNECTION

ORGANIZATIONAL STORYTELLING:

A LEADERSHIP CONNECTION

A story begins, as so many do, with a journey.

DR. LINDA ELLINGTON

Archway Publishing books may be ordered through booksellers or by contacting:

Archway Publishing
1663 Liberty Drive
Bloomington, IN 47403
www.archwaypublishing.com
844-669-3957

ISBN: 978-1-6657-6751-4 (sc)
ISBN: 978-1-6657-6752-1 (e)

Library of Congress Control Number: 2024922576

Print information available on the last page.

Archway Publishing rev. date: 10/18/2024

PREFACE

The universe is made of stories, not atoms

Poet Muriel Rukeyser

Inspiration for books comes from myriad sources. In my case, something more than intellectual curiosity excited me about this project—personally. I wrote this book because I recognized that stories are comforting, exhilarating, and unnerving and are part of the fabric of who I am—and who you are.

This book hopefully inspires a new generation of leaders to break free from the monotony of spreadsheets and pie charts. Instead, the stories empower them with the transformative power of storytelling that illuminates organizational missions, values, and goals. Each chapter is a treasure trove brimming with storytelling gems, inviting you on a storytelling odyssey. It is like embarking on a quest to uncover the secrets of legendary leaders and storytellers who harnessed the power of stories to conquer challenges.

As a leader who tells stories, you may notice people throughout the organization looking at you with curiosity. This is a good sign. You are not the typical leader who bores their audience. Instead, you lead in a vibrant, humor-filled environment where politics is absent in a human (i.e., imperfect) enterprise. Embrace the joy of storytelling and watch as your audience becomes more engaged and enthusiastic.

Throughout the book, this journey of stories gives instances to showcase some of the greatest storytellers. Each is different and yields a unique insight, yet they share a common thread: storytelling. The book paints a vivid picture of what you will experience when meeting those who have transformed into storytelling maestros. I extend a call to action - join the ranks of those who have mastered the art and science of storytelling.

If you notice phrases, ideas, and anecdotes that closely resemble those that appear throughout this book, it is not a matter of sloppy editing. I am repeating myself. I am reshuffling words, hoping to say something exactly right – a work in progress on a storyteller's progress.

This book is intentionally written as a 'short story' for two reasons. First, I do not know if anyone has time to read a lengthy book in our chaotic world. Secondly, this book is built on the stories told by storytellers who have been and still are contributing to the field. If you do not already know many of the fantastic storytellers in this book, you will never forget them. Many leadership books might be "Moby Dick' compared to my 'Pilot Fish' book here – but I welcome you to enjoy the adventure with me!

Linda

CONTENTS

CHAPTER 1

INTRODUCTION

We all know stories can get people to take action, accelerate knowledge acquisition, engage in organizational change, solidify teamwork relationships, provide exceptional customer service, and increase the organization's visibility. According to Frei & Morris, "When your organization needs to make a significant change, stories will help to convey not only the why but also what the future will look like in specific, vivid terms. Depending on the measurement, up to 70% of organizational change efforts fail. However, creating a compelling narrative will greatly increase the chances of defying those odds" (2023, p. 71).

Storytellers do this. They create moments of unexpected change to seize the attention of their protagonists and, by extension, the readers and listeners. Aristotle argued that peripeteia, a dramatic turning point, is one of the most potent moments in drama (Stor, 2020).

Organizational storytelling is the secret elixir that transforms dry data into thrilling narratives, igniting inspiration and galvanizing teams to conquer the most epic quests in their industry's ever-changing landscape. The ancient art of wielding words, images, and emotions to craft compelling tales brings the organization's purpose, values, and mission to life like a vibrant tapestry of adventure.

Storytelling is a universal way we have communicated since time began and is a highly honed and valued leadership tool. There can be no arguing that we are in a leadership crisis. And not just in politics but in all industries worldwide. Can you remember when a leader shared a story that made you laugh, cry, want to drink a beer, or feel something? Telling stories is as natural and vital as taking a breath.

The very first storytellers were hunters. They told stories about the animals they killed for sustenance and described the mystical world the animals went to when they died. Animals gave life to early man, and man showed respect in return. The hunters' stories reflect the relationship with the animal kingdom (Luhn, 2018). They often emphasize the ethical considerations and rituals involved, underscoring the importance of sustainable practices and the interconnectedness of all living beings. I dare say we still do that!

Storytelling began so long ago that its opening lines have dissolved into the mists of deep time. Early humans crafted remarkably symmetrical hand axes, hunting cooperatively and possibly controlling fire. Such skills would have required careful observation and mimicry, step-by-step instruction, and an ability to hold a long series of events in one's mind incipient form of plot. Possibly much earlier, humans were creating the type of complex, imaginative, and densely populated murals found on the chalky canvases of ancient caves: art that reveals creatures no longer content to experience the world simply but who felt compelled to record and re-imagine it. We became consummate storytellers (Zak, 2013).

I have a story. So do you! Storytelling is, in fact, at the core of every activity and at the center of everything we do. The ability to tell the right story at the right time is an essential leadership skill for maneuvering through a turbulent world. The mind-boggling and extraordinary truth, scholars and practitioners agree that stories work and are contagious. They are vehicles to teach, inspire, inform, motivate, heal, and lead.

For many brilliant leaders who are good at what they do, the idea of organizational storytelling takes much work. Organizations are people, and this flash of the obvious has implications for leaders discovering that they are being called to show up differently. The messy element of emotion characterizes systems with people in them, and for the leader seeking to influence, that requires a specific set of skills. Leaders increasingly turn to one of humanity's oldest communication tools to lead in a world of complexity, uncertainty, and ambiguity. The story is a significant new idea that is not new at all (Hutchens, 2021).

During my 23-year tenure at IBM, I saw leaders make the mistake of treating their organizations as if they were primarily rational systems. Humans are emotional first, then rational. When the schema got stuck, the thought was that people were not moving. They need more data. So, the leaders showed up with slides. The slides! They looked something like this:

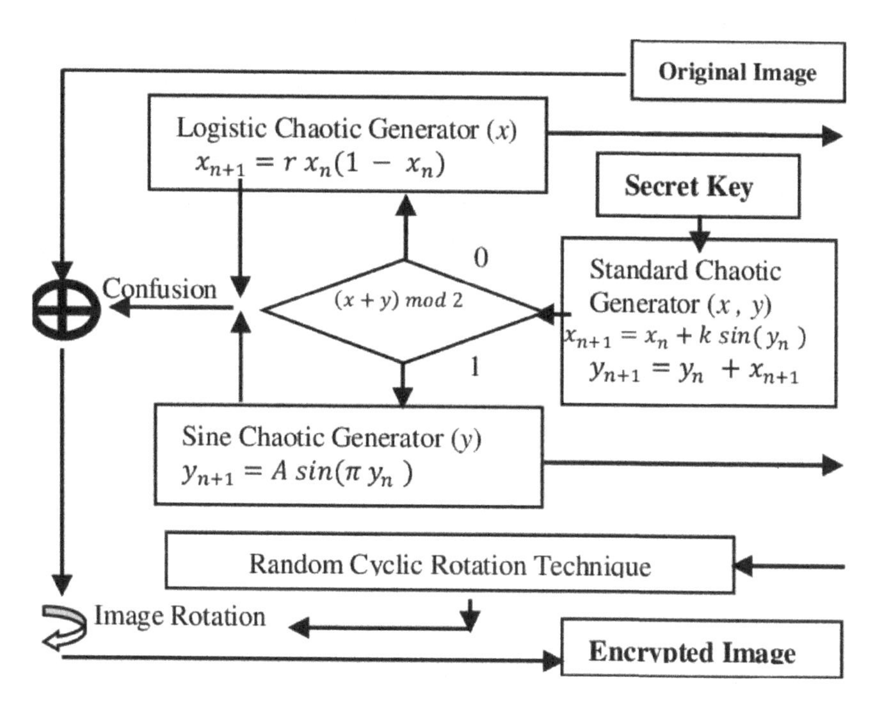

I know I hear you! Painful. Data does not move people, especially in a world that has become noisy. Attempts to influence people with data usually backfire, making people dig in their heels even more. The ways many leaders attempt to unstick their systems typically make them more stuck (Hutchens, 2021). When it comes to data in storytelling, less is more (Frei & Morris, 2023, p. 68).

When you think about the change you want to lead, ask yourself: Can I capture the vision on one page, a paragraph, or a word? The French philosopher Blaise Pascal once apologized for writing a long letter, explaining that he did not have the time to compose a short one (Frei & Morris, 2023, p.66). Your call to action is to create an equivalent of a quick note – even though it may take extra time.

CHAPTER 2

HOW DOES STORYTELLING WORK?

Is there proof that stories work? Is there a single tipping point everyone can point to?

So, what is organizational storytelling? According to David Boje, it is a collective system in which the performance of stories is a vital part of people's sensemaking and a means to allow them to supplement individual memories with institutional memory (2008, p.1). Stories have been delivered across different media throughout recorded history - since Cro-Magnon figured out that mineral pigments like iron oxide and black manganese could be applied to the sides of rocks and caves (Rutledge, 2022). Thus, creating an image chronicling life.

Leaders can inspire others to act like heroes in a story by sharing similar passions and interests. For example, politicians often connect to their audience by highlighting traits we can all relate to, like Bill Clinton playing the saxophone or Ronald Reagan being a fan of jellybeans. Shining a light on their features helps leaders seem more human and connect better with the audience if only to say, *howdy, I am just like you* (Luhn, 2018, p.76). So, sharing interests and passions such as music, food, sports teams, or as large and complex as social or environmental causes can inspire folks to follow your story, hero. The audience stops listening when leaders give up on their dreams and passions. It would be best if you communicated that your hero would keep fighting for what they believe in until the bitter end. Walt Disney once said, "The difference between winning and losing is often not quitting" (Luhn, 2018, p. 78).

This is not 'new' news – storytelling is a powerful tool for communication and engagement, enabling leaders to convey their identity, values, and goals in a way that resonates deeply with their audience. Using storytelling leverages the power of narratives to communicate complex ideas, foster understanding, and build a sense of community. Leaders need to use stories, authentic stories, warts and all. Stories that are vulnerable and honest create a strong relationship by inviting the audience to an experience, not a mission statement. Because in the end, people will forget what you said or did, but they will never forget how you made them feel (Luhn, 2018, p.48). However, if your story falls short of credibility, empathy soon dissipates, and your story loses the listeners' hearts.

Leaders can fail. Storytelling has been documented to have failed for thousands of years. The most beloved leaders are the ones who are vulnerable. They struggle, they fail, and they prevail. Steve Jobs had plenty of struggles. When he was fired from Apple, he purchased the computer graphics division of Lucasfilm and co-founded Pixar. Leaders are decisive. When the chips are down, they make the call. Great leaders do not wait because they know failure will swallow them. They do not hesitate or waffle, even if it is a decision that sometimes does not work out how they had hoped. However, they know they cannot drive the action alone. They need others, such as allies and villains. Leaders say what they feel, ask for help, and call the enemy out when no one else will (Luhn, 2018, p.79). A relatively newer iteration of the use of story is *storydoing*, defined by Ty Montague in his book *True Story: How to Combine Story and Action to Transform Your Business* (2013), brings into reality that the manifestations of an authentic and meaningful story, one told primarily through action, not advertising, are leaders who are storydoers, agile, adaptive to change, and more efficiently run their business.

Is organizational storytelling a *bridge too far* . . . Storytelling is typically used to reference something too ambitious or drastic to be realistic or to describe a very complicated and challenging action to execute. The bridge is not too far if you know that storytelling is a timeless and universal art form that has captivated human imagination for thousands of years. Across cultures and languages, storytelling has been the vessel through which we convey our histories, share our dreams, and explore the depths of creativity. It is a powerful medium that transports us to distant worlds, introduces us to intriguing characters, and imparts valuable lessons. In this age of technology and information, storytelling remains as vital as ever, serving as a bridge between the past and the present, a means to inspire, connect, and communicate the sense of human experience.

Many companies train for communication skills but only sometimes focus on specific skills to communicate ideas about not-yet-existent things. Because the counterfactual, imagined model does not fully exist, it must be embodied in another way to inspire others. This is where stories can be powerful.

Simply passing information to someone is not enough since (1) there is no interest, and nothing is achieved; (2) we are swimming in information, and information alone does not automatically create interest; and (3) we need to be selective because leaders cannot tell it all (Reeves & Fuller, 2021). What is going on when we share an idea? We are not passing an object from one brain to another. We are provoking another brain, hoping the person becomes inspired enough to imagine something similar to what we are imagining. Often, something else is needed. The mental model is an exciting and beautiful castle in the subjective world. When you talk to other people, they might create the equivalent of a palace to be a dingy studio apartment in their mind's eye (Reeves & Fuller, 2021, p.98).

In their book, *The Imagination Machine* (2021), Reeves and Fuller (2021) identify some techniques of compelling storytelling that can be used in enlisting others to help evolve and amplify new ideas:

- Use emotional content: Ms. Peabody talks about being astonished.
- Play to many senses: images, video, evocative description.

- Use specific color and detail rather than generalizations or summaries.
- Incorporate the structure of an archetypal narrative, if possible: A trigger that sets the protagonist off on some journey or struggle.

To become a great storyteller, you should gain familiarity with great stories, not necessarily by quoting them directly but by honing your instincts for description, language choice, and mental imagery. For inspiration, here are a few basic plots throughout human storytelling (Reeves & Fuller, 2021, pp. 101-102.)

- Voyage and return
- Rags to riches
- The quest
- Comedy
- Tragedy
- Rebirth

Storytelling works like an enchanting spell, weaving threads of emotion, purpose, and connection into the organization's fabric. It captures the hearts and minds of your team, making them bold adventurers in the grad saga of the company's journey. The story compass guides you through uncharted waters, the sword that slays doubt and resistance, and the treasure map to unearthing boundless potential. In the thrilling realm of leadership, storytelling is the catalyst that propels your vision beyond the stars, where dreams become realities, and where the future is a story yet to be told – and you, the leader, hold the pen.

CHAPTER 3

OUR BRAIN: THE NARRATIVE ARCHITECT

A remarkable universe is concealed within us in the vast tapestry of human existence – a universe of wonder, imagination, and emotion. It is a place where dreams take flight, memories linger, and the essence of our very being resides. Welcome to the captivating realm of the human brain, the magnificent storyteller of our lives, a labyrinth of neurons and synapses that weave the most intricate and enhancing narratives. With each thought, emotion, and memory, the brain unfolds a unique and enthralling story, painting the canvas of our existence with a palette of vivid experiences. The brain, our extraordinary narrative architect, is where the exceptional tales of our lives are written in the language of neurons and dreams. "Our species thinks in metaphors and learns through stories" (Bateson, as written in Frei and Morris, 2023, p.65).

How can something as simple as a story be so assertive? To understand that, we need to travel to the source of where stories begin in the teller and to the place where they find their home in the receiver – the brain.

The biology of the mind in the twenty-first century is what the biology of the genes was in the twentieth century (Hardiman, 2012, p.1). Stories are how we are wired. Stories take place in the imagination. To the human brain, imagined experiences are processed like real experiences. Stories create genuine emotions, presence (the sense of being somewhere), and behavioral response (Rutledge, 2011). According to Shane Jones, storytelling is one of the most unifying elements of humankind, central to human existence, taking place in every known culture in the world (2017).

As it turns out, the story was crucial to our evolution—more than opposable thumbs (Cron, 2012, p.1). The story is what makes us human, not just metaphorically but literally. Recent breakthroughs in neuroscience reveal that our brain is hardwired to respond to stories; the pleasure we derive from a tale well told is nature's way of seducing us into paying attention to it (Cron, 2012, p.1).

According to Paul Armstrong (2020), narratives take up prefigured aspects of experience, including culturally shared conventions, assumptions, and practices, and then reconfigure them into as-if- patterns of various kinds (Once up a time…they lived happily ever after…). The experience of reading or listening to a story may prompt the recipient to reconfigure their understanding of the world, and the cycle can then begin again through which storytellers and audiences shape, exchange, and reshape their experiences (p.2).

In their research, Martinez-Conde et al.(2019) found that stories play in our mind's theater, in which the part of a language network in the brain becomes constantly activated when people listen to stories. They say that part of our pleasure from engaging with narratives is their potential to evoke mental images. We do not just process the words and sentences on a page, but we can experience what happens in the story vividly by mentally simulating the content of the narrative (Martinez-Conde et al., 2019, pp. 8285-8290). In a study by Paul Zak, he observed a fantastic neural ballet in which a storyline changed the activity of peoples' brains – neurochemical oxytocin on the move (2014, p.1).

In many ways, stories are uncannily similar to living organisms. They compel us to share them; once told, they grow and change, often becoming longer and more elaborate. They compete for our attention to reach as many minds as possible. They find each other, intermingle, and multiply (Jabr, 2019).

The brain creates a world for us to live in and populates it with allies and villains. It turns the chaos and bleakness of reality into a simple, hopeful tale, and at the center, it places its star – us, who set a series of goals that become the plots of our lives. The story is what the brain does (Stor, 2020, p. 3). In his book, *The Science of Storytelling*, Stor writes about psychologist Professor Jonathan Haidt, who posited that the brain is a story processor, not a logic processor (2020). The story emerges from human minds as naturally as breath emerges between human lips.

Storytelling helps us realize that the biggest, scariest, most painful, or regretful things get small and surmountable when we share them with others. Matthew Dicks reminds us that we are all disappearing – you, me, and everyone we know and love. Thus, when we tell stories, we do ourselves a favor by writing our name in the wet cement of life before we head to whatever is next. It is like leaving a note in the logbook on the trail that others will be hiking after we do, a message that might give the next hiker a clue (Dicks, 2018, p.xii). We are the cave dwellers warning about the ferocious tiger!

According to Susan Weischenk, we use more of our brains when listening to a story (2014). Why is that? Why does the format of a story, where events unfold one after the other, have such a profound impact on us? If broken down into the simplest form, the story is a connection of cause and effect. That is precisely how we think. Because we have a more decadent brain event, we enjoy the experience, understand the information more deeply, and retain it longer (Weischenk, 2014).

According to Nancy Kirsner (2017) from the Whole Being Institute, at least four things are going on in the brain during storytelling :

Cortex Activity: A well-told story engages motor, sensory, and frontal cortexes.

Dopamine Release: When the brain experiences an emotionally charged event, dopamine is released. This makes it easier to remember the event and ensures greater accuracy in memory.

Mirroring (mirror neurons): Listeners have brain activity similar to that of the storyteller and each other.

Neural Coupling: A story activates parts of the brain that, due to neuroplasticity, allow listeners to weave the narrative into their own experiences.

In his essay "The Science of Storytelling: What Listening to a Story Does to Our Brains," entrepreneur and storyteller Leo Widrich noted that when we hear a story, not only are the language processing parts in our brain activated, but any other area in our brain that we would use when experiencing the events of the story is also activated (as written in Peterson, 2017).

So, who are we, if not just a brain?

To be a person is to have a story to tell (Simmons, 2019, p.1). All of us tell stories about ourselves. Stories define us. To know someone well is to know their story – the experiences that have shaped us, the trials and turning points that have tested us. By story, we do not mean something made up to make a bad situation look good. Instead, it talks about profoundly authentic and engaging accounts that listeners feel have a stake in the success (Ibarra & Kent, 2005, p.1). Denning (2011) echoes the same idea: the storyteller should be so engaged with the story – visualizing the action, regarding what the characters feel – that the listeners become drawn into the narrative world (Bateson, 2011, p.21).

Do not forget that an organization has its own story – its founding myth. An effective way to communicate transcendent purpose is by sharing that tale. What passion led the founder(s) to risk health and wealth to start the enterprise? Why was it so important, and what barriers had to be overcome? These are the stories that stay core to the organization's DNA.

Organizational DNA storytelling is a powerful and transformative approach to sharing a company's culture. It is the art of weaving the company's core values, history, and mission into compelling narratives that inform and inspire. Just as DNA carries an individual's genetic code, this form of storytelling encapsulates the genetic makeup of an organization, reflecting its identity, purpose, and character. By harnessing the art of organizational DNA storytelling, companies can foster a sense of belonging and loyalty, ultimately shaping a more unified and engaged community. It is a dynamic tool for crafting the company's stories, fostering a shared culture, and propelling the organization forward with passion and authenticity.

CHAPTER 4

THE PSYCHOLOGY OF STORYTELLING

The psychology of storytelling is a captivating field that delves into the intricate and profound ways human minds engage with narratives. At its core, it explores the cognitive, emotional, and social aspects of how stories influence our thoughts, emotions, and behavior. From childhood bedtime tales to blockbuster movies, from gripping novels to persuasive marketing campaigns, stories have an innate power to capture our attention, connect with our deepest emotions, and shape our understanding of the world.

Understanding the psychology of storytelling unravels the mystery of why stories hold such a universal and timeless appeal. It sheds light on the mechanisms that make narratives memorable, relatable, and persuasive. This knowledge has far-reaching applications, from enhancing educational methods and marketing strategies to informing therapeutic approaches and shaping cultural norms.

In this chapter, we journey through how stories work their magic on the human mind. If we agree that the mental models we live by today are constructed, then they are full of construction materials to be dismantled, altered, and recombined. What does that look like? One idea might be:

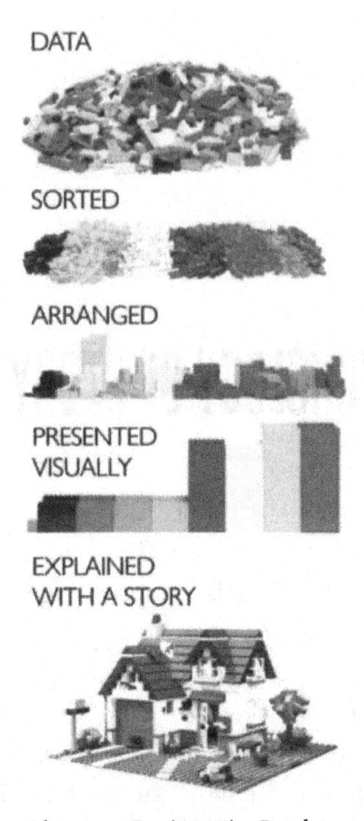

Source: Abramo, L. (2017), *Bridging the PM Competency Gap*. J. Ross Publishing.

A few aspects of storytelling psychology (Rutledge, 2011).

Sense-making and identity: Stories help us make sense of the world and our place in it. They can shape our beliefs, values, and identity. Cultural narratives, such as myths, legends, and religious stories, play a significant role in defining a group's collective identity and values.

Catharsis and healing: Sharing personal stories and listening to others' stories can have therapeutic benefits.

Motivation and goal achievement: Stories often feature characters who face challenges and overcome obstacles. These narratives can inspire and motivate individuals to pursue their goals and persevere in adversity.

Neurological basis: Neuroscience research has shown that our brains are wired for storytelling. When we hear a story, our brains activate in a way that mirrors the characters' experiences. This neural mirroring helps us understand the characters' emotions and actions.

Cultural and individual variability: The impact of storytelling can vary across cultures and individuals. Cultural narratives and storytelling traditions differ worldwide; personal preferences for specific stories or genres can vary widely.

There are a few psychological reasons why stories move us to act (Rutledge, 2011):

A primal form of communication: Stories are timeless links to ancient traditions, legends, archetypes, myths, and symbols. They connect us to a larger self and universal truths.

Overcoming defenses and differences: Stories allow us to understand ourselves better and find commonalities with others.

How we think: Stories are how we make meaning in life. Call them schemas, scripts, cognitive maps, mental models, metaphors, or narratives.

Trigger our imagination: By engaging our imagination, we participate in the narrative.

Incorporating psychology into your organizational storytelling can help create a deeper emotional connection with your audience, foster a sense of belonging, and inspire action. Remember that the key genuinely resonates with your audience's psychological needs and emotions while remaining authentic to your organizational values.

CHAPTER 5

THE STICKINESS FACTOR

There is a scientific reason why stories stick in our minds. In our evolution, when humans developed the ability to speak, they communicated about life-or-death situations, like being chased by a tiger, successfully hunting a bison, or avoiding poisonous plants. We know that storytelling was essential to our early ancestors because we have storyboards of those life lessons painted on cave walls that date back thousands of years. The ancient people who learned those story lessons lived, and those who did not probably met the tiger.

Stories are sticky. A well-told tale 'sticks' to our brains and attaches to our emotions. A speaker can tell a story so that the audience 'sees' the story in their mind's eye and 'feels' the story's emotions. In some situations, an audience may become so involved in the story that they react by making facial expressions or gasping in surprise. The audience is moved from being a passive listener to an active participant by seeing the story and physically reacting to it.

Mead (2021) illustrates the connection between feeling and doing:

- Imagine you are looking at the Eiffel Tower.
- Think of two words that start with w.

- Imagine that I am cutting a lemon in half and then squeezing the juice into a glass.
- Imagine fingernails running down a chalkboard.

Stephen Denning suggests telling stories that are in harmony with the voices in people's heads (2011). You do not want your audience to ignore their voice; you like to tell a story that awakens their voice to tell its own story. You awaken their voice, and then you give it something to do. Denning advocates using stories as springboards to help the audience think of situations so they can begin to solve problems mentally. In this way, you are not speaking to an audience, but rather, you are inviting them to participate with you.

Stickiness and the Shift

The irresistible power of a story is a perfectly placed, impeccably delivered story that transports a person to a place beyond interest, straight past paying attention, and into a state of complete captivation. A shift happens in us, a change in our understanding, a shift in our desires (Hall, 2019, pp. 10-12). The shift a story can make has a profound impact on business. It turns customers into converts. It transforms employees into evangelists. Executives into leaders. It changes the nature and effect of marketing, and perhaps most importantly, it can change how we see ourselves (Hall, 2019, p. xvi.). Companies whose cultures wither instead of thriving are affected by their leaders' inability to articulate the stories of why they do what they do. There is good news: no magic is required. Leaders only need to discover how storytelling can change how everyone in the business thinks, feels, and behaves.

For those in the presence of story and storytelling in its purest form, there is a power that effortlessly includes three elements: attention, influence, and transformation. In Kendra Hall's book *Stories that Stick* (2019, pp. 10-12), she describes those elements that help build the bridge from the storyteller to the audience:

Attention: Storytelling is an experience of losing oneself in a story called narrative transportation. Even when genuinely transported into a novel, we lose awareness of our immediate surroundings. For example, if you have ever missed your exit while listening to a story-driven podcast or audiobook, you understand the effects of narrative transportation all too well. In that moment, did you feel coerced into surrendering your attention? No. You traveled willingly into the world of the story. At this point, engagement metamorphizes into something much more valuable: captivation.

Influence: With a story, resistance dissipates. With a story, we do not need to taste the food to want to go to the restaurant. A level allows people to fall in love with the product, appreciate the value of the service, and then feel compelled to act. We are willing participants and work on our desires.

Transformation: We know that a story can transport the listener into the world of that story (attention). We understand that the more engrossed an audience is in a story, the more likely they are to adopt the perspectives within the narrative (influence). Once the audience emerges from the story, they are changed. And not just for a minute or two; the effects are long-lasting.

However, beware, there is a danger of storytelling stickiness that incorporates moral claims, even when they are inaccurate facts, shifting listener beliefs, values, and sense of self. Through polished rhetorical style and resource control strategies with tacitly or explicitly supportive workplace contents, leaders can construct convincing but morally disengaged narratives that violate ethical principles and yield moral ambiguity by excluding, marginalizing, and disfiguring the story (Dzurec, 2020).

Understanding the world is shaped by a hunger for a narrative that arises from ambiguity and arbitrary events. We strive to fit the events of our lives into a cohesive story that accounts for our circumstances, the things that occur, and our choices. Each of us has a different narrative, woven into it from our shared culture and experience of being human and many distinct threads that explain the singular events of one's past (Brown et al., 2014). All these experiences influence what comes to mind in a current situation and the narrative through which we make sense. In this way, narrative and memory become one. History provides meaning and a framework for imbuing future experiences and information with purpose, shaping new memories to fit our established construct of the world and ourselves. The success of a magician or politician, like that of a novelist, relies on the seductive powers of narrative and the audience's willing suspension of disbelief.

Brown et al. (2014) highlight that illusions can come from storytelling. This can be akin to imagination inflation, which refers to the tendency of people who, when asked through a story to imagine an event, will often begin to believe, when questioned about it later, that the event occurred. Isn't this what leaders do when they try to get buy-in for a vision they developed? Another type of illusion is caused by suggestion, which may arise simply in how a question is asked during storytelling. Be aware that there is a danger if you embed leading questions with your stories. The power of inflation in storytelling can move markets and underpin reality – thus causing infrastructural chaos and uncertainty.

While stories cannot solve all organizational issues, they can make a real impact on the life of an organization. When clearly articulating the distinctive attributes of compelling storytelling, the applications of storytelling are endless. However, in the application of storytelling, be smart. I know many leaders who have blunted their effectiveness by relentlessly parading their brains (a.k.a. being a smart-ass), especially when the leader is on the stage. The employees in the audience are more talented as a group than the storyteller. Learn to tell the story – this is not about you, the leader.

CHAPTER 6

STORYTELLING AS AN ART

Storytelling is a multifaceted art form transcending time and culture. In the context of art, storytelling brings art to life (Trinkoff, 2015). Although our fast-paced electronic society does not always nurture the art of storytelling, telling stories can be an empowering remedy for healing alienation. Instead of humanizing technologies while dehumanizing ourselves, storytelling embraces the essence of person-to-person communication, weaving a sense of personal and collective welfare within organizations (Lawrence & Paige, 2016).

In an age when global corporations are getting even more prominent, business models are evolving faster, and artificial intelligence is changing how we work. Companies need storytelling more than ever. Rather than treating storytelling as an unruly art, leaders can systematically cultivate and harness it. To create great organizations, leaders need to see and create things that have never existed and a mechanism to trigger employees' imagination – and they do this through stories.

Storytelling and leadership are both performance arts and like other performance arts, they involve at least as much doing as thinking. Moreover, organizational stories do not need to fit a well-made story's pattern like art. For instance, a springboard story that communicates a complex idea and sparks actions generally needs a plot and a turning point. A narrative that shares knowledge about problems, solutions, and explanations often needs a hero or heroine (Denning, 2011).

Depree states that when we think about leaders and the variety of gifts people bring to corporations and institutions, we see that the art of leadership lies in polishing, liberating, and enabling those gifts—storytelling (2011). Storytelling is one of the few ways to handle leadership's most essential and complex challenges: sparking action, getting people to work together, and leading people into the future.

Bullet points in a presentation are boring. The brain is set up to listen to a story. That is why sports are more exciting than science. They have a beginning, a middle, and an end. Science has data and information – but scientists do not tell stories. Everyone needs to tell a story of whatever they are trying to accomplish. Storytelling is a simple formula, and you do not require a scientific glass funnel.

You do not need to be a superhero to tell great stories. Choy shared his story:

> I benefited from the wisdom of storytelling and screenwriting guru Robert McKee. His former students have included more than sixty Academy Award winners. "Given the choice between trivial material brilliantly told versus profound material poorly told, an audience will always choose the trivial told brilliantly (2017, p.xx).

Most people like Choy and myself, and probably you, are not born master storytellers or designed to be world-renowned superheroes. However, we can tell great stories.

As my artist friends explain, art is utterly incomprehensive and is, therefore, full of deep significance. So, lighten up. If you are not an artist, you can be that brilliant storyteller!

CHAPTER 7

STORYTELLING IS IN THE ORGANIZATION'S DNA

The bedrock of culture is built by people identifying with the values through stories. Building a culture begins by inviting the soul to work. Essex and Mainemelis (2002) share a comment written by Whyte in 1994, which is noteworthy for this chapter:

> As the fire of our creativity burns its way into our interior life as much as it transforms the world at large, we experience what the medieval philosophers called the alchemical wedding, the meeting of the interior world of a single human being with the great soul of the world. The betwixt-and-between world is the very touchstone of creativity. It exists as much in a development plan as in a great canvas.

Storytelling is in an organization's DNA.

We could discuss the legacy story itself. In a Western sense, legacy is the mark a person leaves on history. Statues are raised for heroes, for those who are revered. However, many cultures see that differently. Very little is known about how storytelling organizations differ, how they work, how they respond to their environment, how to change them, and how to survive in them. Even less is known about the insider's view of the storytelling organization, its theater of everyday life. When you work, you become known for your story, promoted, and fired for your story. It is not always the story you want to be told, but there are ways to change and re-story it (Boje, 2008).

Organizational storytelling is not about fairy tales or traditional stories told to children. It involves the sorts of stories that are told every day throughout the organization by those who want to achieve real-world objectives. For example, Godin spins a silly tale about uniqueness, speculating that brown cows are boring after you have seen one, two, or ten (2002). A purple cow, though, would be something! Storytelling could be the purple cow: phenomenal, counterintuitive, exciting, and remarkable. Every day, people ignore a lot of brown cows, but they will not overlook a purple cow.

This may seem hardly worth mentioning; however, those unfamiliar with the art of storytelling may be reading this, questioning the purpose of the cow analogy and wondering about the unfamiliarity of telling stories as leaders. In *Poetics*, an ancient Greek text is credited as a functional influence on Western storytelling - Aristotle referred to storytelling as recognition or a change from ignorance to knowledge (Bronstein, 2016). With stories, people share the same space and feel a sense of togetherness. Stories are linked to a feeling of active participation and co-creation on the part of the audience. When you tell the right story, others feel involved, as opposed to having been performed at. They can put themselves in the action of the story. The listeners become the story's heroes, which can, in turn, affect their roles in the real world, so they are not extras in the scenery of life.

Garmston would tell the leaders who are somewhat afraid to tell stories, thinking you as the leader would be distracted and worried by inactive or scowling participants in the audience, which renderers the leader less effective – is to know that those fears are dead wrong (2019, p. xix).

In Garmston's own words:

> "The moment I began to tell stories, my own and those I had heard from others, audience members perked up and began to attend with laser intensity, and I started to have more fun. So did the audience and groups I led in my role as leader. And I suspect they carried away more in their hearts and minds. To begin the journey of using a story or advance to new levels of effectiveness, all that is necessary is to try." (2019, p.xiii)

Storytelling is ageless and is the currency of human relationships. Humans naturally gravitate toward great storytellers because they are the most interesting people. They elevate people's consciousnesses and inspire creative people to believe in the power of their dreams. Stories are vibrant forms of expression that bring life and meaning to every human activity. The belief that storytelling is necessary and beneficial for our times has the power to spark a renaissance.

When organizational leaders develop their core story, they communicate their purpose and values and display authentic meaning that others can believe in, participate in, and share. This is the basis for cultural and social change within the organization and across societies (Rutledge, 2011).

Storytelling should exist in every organization. Storytelling is now at the forefront of many business conversations, Microsoft, Verizon, Nike, and Boeing have all created the role of Chief Storyteller. United Airlines, one of the most recent companies to design and develop this position, hired a new 'crew member' to fulfill that role. A recent Adidas job ad listed storytellers among those they are seeking to hire for the store manager position (Garmston, 2019, p. xxv).

When organizational leaders take the time to develop and communicate their core story, they are doing much more than sharing information about their business. They are articulating a more profound sense of purpose, embedding the organization's values into a cohesive narrative that reflects its mission and long-term goals. This core story serves as a beacon of authenticity, providing a framework for employees, customers, and other stakeholders to resonate with, believe in, and rally around.

A well-developed core story gives people something to connect with emotionally, allowing them to feel part of something larger than themselves. It moves beyond facts and figures to convey the organization's identity in a relatable, meaningful, and human way. Leaders invite participation by engaging others with this authentic narrative, fostering a culture where individuals feel aligned with the organization's values and vision. This shared sense of purpose strengthens internal cohesion and enhances brand loyalty and trust among external audiences.

Moreover, a strong core story helps the organization navigate challenges and adapt to market changes by focusing on the "why" behind the business. It becomes a guiding principle for decision-making, enabling leaders to maintain consistency in their messaging, strategy, and behavior, even in times of uncertainty. As people share in this story and become advocates for the organization's mission, they contribute to the long-term success and sustainability of the business.

Ultimately, crafting and communicating a compelling core story enables leaders to build deeper connections, inspire action, and create a legacy that transcends profits, allowing their organization to thrive on purpose-driven growth.

CHAPTER 8

THE TEXTURE OF A STORY

Those who lead will enhance their persuasiveness through a storytelling repertoire (Garmston, 2019). The word *nkali* loosely translates to be greater than another. Like our economic and political worlds, stories are also defined by the principle of nkali: how they are told, who tells them, when they are told, and how many narratives are told are dependent on power. The single story creates stereotypes; the problem with stereotypes is not that they are untrue but incomplete. They make one story become the only story. Stories have been used to dispossess and to malign, but stories can also be utilized to empower and humanize. Stories can break a person's dignity, but stories can also repair that broken dignity. That philosophy is the driving force in telling a story. What will stand out is your intentionality. Susman (2023) states that intentionality plays a significant role in leadership mindset. It is easy to recognize those who are driven by a singular intention. We see it in their eyes. We hear it in their voices. Their mission is present. There are no talking points, only a deeply held belief, a persistent point to make (Susman, 2023). Do your due diligence, and do not assume anything. Highlight the gaps that need to be filled in and do so with a *tinogona spirit* (Susman, 2023).

Soft, fuzzy, emotional, anecdotal, fantasy, fairy tales, primitive, childish – these terms advocate conventional leadership used to describe organizational storytelling. Traditional established leaders see it as contaminating the world of pure reason with the poison of emotions and feelings, thereby dragging society back into the dark ages. It takes a certain amount of intellectual courage to suggest that the world of rational leadership might have much to learn from the ancient narrative tradition. Wage the war against corporate speak. A question to ask folks is, "Am I boring you?"

Go ahead, picture yourself telling the organization's story, even if it is a fuzzy picture. Then, perform your script with derring-do. Does it sound wild? Silly? Naïve? Maybe, but it is not. We all know that the first 99.9 percent of getting from here to there is the determination to do it and not to compromise, no matter what roadblocks are erected around us. If you are confronted with a roadblock, consider yourself a bumper car. You bump, back up, or turn around and go in another direction. There is a story to be told – tell it. The basics of leadership storytelling can be mastered quickly. Mastery of the discipline, however, takes a lifetime.

Yes, it will be messy. Good stories start messy, unclear, unimpressive – even ugly. A leader might be allergic to storytelling or feel too high in the leadership hierarchy to engage in a seemingly frivolous creative pursuit. Or are you the leader who is confused and intimidated, who thinks storytelling is for the experts – the songwriters, poets, the kind of people whose every word keeps you on the edge of your seat? Or, at the opposite end of the spectrum, and far more problematic, are the self-proclaimed natural-born storytellers – is that you? Often, these leaders think that an inspirational quote from Steve Jobs or Mahatma Gandhi, for instance, is a story. Or a customer testimonial in and of itself is a story. Stories – real stories – contain certain fundamental, timeless elements that give them power. Ignore those fundamentals at your peril. You could end up squandering an opportunity to change minds and lives (Biesenbach (2018). Storytelling is an ongoing project of revising and reimagining with no clear beginning or end. Instead, it is a project worth doing at any leadership level. Practice your art of storytelling so it can become part of your texture.

You may be asking yourself why you should be a storyteller. Everyone understands the story. People identify with the values in stories, which builds an organization's texture. The story is everlasting. Like fire, when it is not blazing, it is smoldering under its ashes or sleeping inside its flint house.

Stories define us, not language. Although it is often said that language defines us, dolphins, whales, and elephants have language, as far as we know, they do not have stories. Or do they?

Leaders who get promoted to increasingly higher levels of leadership are those who tell compelling and inspirational stories. John Hennessy, Stanford's 10th President, sees this as an essential skill for bringing people together and unifying them to a single vision. However, he says such leadership skills do not happen independently; thus, they must be developed (Garmston, 2019).

Stories are more than dramas people tell or read. As a pattern, stories are a powerful way of organizing and sharing individual experiences and exploring and co-creating realities. Our psyches and cultures are filled with narratives of influence, shaping individuals' and collectives' awareness and behavior (Atlee, n/d). The story is woven into the fabric of the universe, which is more profound and durable than matter itself. The poet Muriel Rukeyser, says that the universe is made of stories, not atoms (Rukeyser, 1968).

Results from a dozen prominent cognitive scientists and developmental psychologists have confirmed that human minds rely on stories and story architecture as the primary roadmap for understanding, making sense of, remembering, and planning our lives and the countless experiences and narratives we encounter (Haven, 2007). Haven's research shows evidence that stories are efficient and effective structural vehicles to motivate, teach, and communicate factual, conceptual, and tacit information (attitudes, beliefs, values, and cultural expectations) (2007, p. viii).

Storytelling is significant in value by asking questions. Are stories important? How can stories help organizations be not only successful but also sustainable? How can a leader tell a story with impact? One answer to those questions is that the power of stories illustrates a vital message that, as a leader, a key role you have is to seek out moments to make heroes of others and to maintain consistency in telling the story of the path and progress to all stakeholders. The storyteller, if practical, does not dictate the organization's direction. The storyteller describes a new perspective through the story and raises excitement about the organizational journey. Though intangible, stories have something solid that helps maintain a sense of commitment. A good story is a significant foundation for everyone in the organization.

CHAPTER 9

BE THE MASTER OF YOUR STORYTELLING

In a speech to the House of Commons on September 9, 1941, Winston Churchill paraphrased the last two lines of a short poem, I*nvictus*, written by Willian Henley in 1875:

> *We are the masters of our fate. We are the captains of our souls.*

Leaders who are struggling to be organizational storytellers, lighten up! Folks trust people who put their feet up, spout an occasional four-letter word, and laugh at their screw-ups.

In his TED Talk, Majeed Mogharreban describes the traits essential to excellent leadership storytelling (2018). He believes that stories have the power to change the world. His formula is simple: Leaders need to transport people from 'pain island' to 'pleasure island,' and they do this with their 'boat.' One of his examples was Martin Luther King, Jr. *I Have a Dream* speech. The pain island was slavery. The pleasure island ended racism and the beginning of equality for all people. His boat was the Civil Rights Movement.

Pain Island **The Boat** **Pleasure Island**

Source: Mogharreban TEDx SunValley

You need not to limit yourself to words. When Jan Carlzon led Scandinavian Airlines' turnaround in the 1980s, he circulated a small, illustrated pamphlet featuring a sad cartoon plane to convey the company's switch to a strategy anchored in delighting business travels. This simple act was widely embraced by everyone and helped the leaders chart a course through turbulence and change (Frei & Morriss, 2023). When telling organizational stories, use words, numbers, cartoons, and pictures – all of which bring the story to life.

In Denning's 2011 book, *The Leader's Guide to Storytelling*, Bateson created a storytelling catalog for leaders who should employ a variety of narrative patterns for different aims:

- Sparking action.
- Communicate who you and the organization are.
- Fostering collaboration.
- Taming the rumor mill.
- Sharing knowledge.
- Leading people into the future.

Boris and Peterson (2018) are proponents of leaders building a storytelling culture. This encourages everyone to listen for, think, and tell stories that yield many benefits. They propose a way to ensure that all levels of the organization capture the story moments:

- Have leaders role models by sharing their stories.
- Mentors and coaches should share their experiences through stories and encourage the stories of those they are guiding.

- Encourage employees to capture their work and report their progress in a story.
- Place listening to stories and sharing great stories at the center of each leader's agenda.

Lwin (2010, p.368) identified the fundamental features of spontaneous, synchronized gestures and facial expressions. In the *Language and Literature Journal* article, Lwin writes about the suggested method of oral storytelling as a semiotic method, which considers the relation of gesture form to meaning and function, i.e., typology. This work classified the typology into four major types:

Mimic gestures: Movements of the hands, arms, and the rest of the body have a close formal relationship to the semantic content of speech.

Metaphoric gestures: Representational gestures mimic gestures but correspond to an abstract idea, not to a concrete object or event, e.g., using two hands to depict the scales of justice when saying 'decide.'

Beat: Rhythmical movements of the hand according to pulsations of speech, indexing the word or phrase it accompanies as significant.

Deictic gestures: Points indicating objects around the teller or abstract pointing, i.e., the gesture space, may look empty, but to the teller, it is a field with discourse entities.

According to the 2022 International Storytelling Festival,

> Throughout the world, in every culture, people have told stories – at home and work, when the harvest was taken in, the wood was cut and carted, and the wool was woven. And while the folks were telling their stories, so too were the bards and minstrels, the griots and troubadours, the poets, singers, and guardians of a people's history.

Dr. Trent tells the story of a native South African culture with a particular way of greeting strangers and familiar people that recognizes the essence of the moment, not 'hello' but a more profound interaction of *ubuntu*. Their cultural greeting expresses the power of collectiveness, acknowledging and giving space to each other's joy, pain, and dignity (2017, p.189).

Current leaders may want to begin their storytelling by greeting people with *Sawubona*, which means "I see you." This greeting from South African culture magnifies shared humanity and affirms that we are inextricably connected in ways beyond human understanding and that our survival is dependent on one another. Leaders then show a sense of building authentic relationships based on the power of our collectiveness and the gift found in our oneness. Isn't this how we should show up in the world of leadership?

CHAPTER 10

STORYTELLING IS A COMPETITIVE ADVANTAGE

Matthew Dicks tells us that storytelling is remarkable because when you tell a story, people remember what you said (2018). You have been shown one million bar graphs throughout your life. How many bar graphs do you remember right now? When was the last time you said, you know, that PowerPoint deck? Would you show that one to me again? When did you say, could I take that pie graph home? I want to show my friends this excellent pie graph. Do we remember data? We do remember stories.

The best story wins (Luhn, 2018). Storytelling is a strategy. Stories are relevant, stories are evolving, and stories are yours. These words, emblazoned across your mind and soul, constitute leadership's modus operandi. Your job is to capture the dynamics in an oral storytelling performance that is aesthetic and communicatively effective. Your performance is an interplay between verbal, vocal, and visual features of the story that produces specific interpretations and meanings of the events and characters in the story.

At the heart of leadership lies persuasion. At the heart of persuasion lies storytelling. Whether you know it or not, you engage in both daily. Whatever industry you are in, you are competing. Your competitors may not even be people but other companies, funding priorities, or endless perfect substitutions to what you are offering. You are also competing constantly for attention with other things that demand people's attention, mostly their phone screens (Choy, 2017).

Organizational storytelling can substantially impact a company's bottom line, contributing to its financial success and overall performance. Luhn (2018) provides simple steps to becoming a great storyteller and, thus, influencing the bottom line:

- We crave stories because they give voice to what we want and believe in. Through storytelling, we express our desires and our fears.
- The memories we retain are connected to a compelling story.
- Share funny, happy, or suspenseful stories to create high levels of dopamine or endorphins and sad or melancholy stories to develop high levels of oxytocin. Include satisfying and tragic moments in your story to keep your audience on the edge of their seats.
- Great stories are not just for entertainment but also for creating successful businesses and brands. Do some of your favorite companies or brands have a memorable story?
- Tell the stories that are the beating heart under the surface of your organization.

What is the impact if storytelling is set free to speak for itself?

Leaders may be allergic to telling stories because they need help finding them or think they have to present data and that there is no room to tell a story. Tell your story whenever the opportunity arises: in speeches, interviews, town hall meetings, team huddles, and one-on-one (Frei & Morriss, 2023).

Storytelling is a critical skill for a leader because telling a story makes people trust you more. What makes a great story? Eber (2021) states that the story will ask these three questions:

1. What is the context, meaning what is the setting, who is involved, and why should I care?
2. What is the conflict's meaning, and what is that moment when everything changes?
3. What is the outcome, meaning, where is it different, and what is the takeaway?

Joseph Campbell's book, *The Hero With a Thousand Faces,* continues to profoundly influence creative artists, including authors, songwriters, game designers, filmmakers, and leaders (2008). His book inspires all those interested in the inherent human need to tell stories. Campbell knew that to impact his craft of storytelling, he needed to travel extensively, even into the jungles around the world. His curiosity led him to uncover myths and folktales from every corner of the world, and he learned to let the stories speak for themselves, to let teachings from stories be heard and talked about.

An example of a story that speaks for itself is when Campbell describes the *Spot of the Buddha* legend, in which the world may be said to revolve:

> Beneath this spot is the earth-supporting head of the cosmic serpent, the dragon, symbolic of the waters of the abyss, which are the divine life-creative energy and substance of the demiurge, the world-generative aspect of immortal beings. From that springs the *World Navel,* a symbol of continuous creation, the mystery of maintaining the world through that constant ongoing miracle of vivification, e.g., animate, which swells within all things. (2008, p.32)

Let us stay with mythology here for a moment. Did you know Kokopelli is an icon of the Pueblo Hopi people? He is often referred to as a 'mythical storyteller.' Did he evolve as a whimsical symbol of the Pueblo culture? Or was he a natural person? Did he travel from village to village, entertaining with his flute day by day and telling stories at night? No one knows. However, a Hopi Nation proverb says that those who tell stories rule the world (Golden, 2013).

Say hello to Suzanne Simard.

Like Campbell, Suzanne Simard realized that to build her storytelling craft, she needed to have the ability to intentionally hear many voices – words of wisdom from the forest. In her book, *Finding the Mother Tree*, she provides an analogy of organizations:

> "Nothing lives on our planet without death and decay. From this springs new life, and from this birth will come new death. The spiral of living taught me to become a sower of seeds, a planter of seedlings, a keeper of saplings, and a part of the cycle. The forest is part of much larger cycles: the building of soil, the migration of species, and the circulation of oceans—the source of clean air, pure water, and good food. There is necessary wisdom and the give-and-take of nature – its quiet agreements and search for balance. There is extraordinary generosity." (2021, p.3)

I learned about Suzanne Simard when, through her written words, she took me with her to discover the wisdom of the forest. Like Campbell, she realized that to build her storytelling craft, she needed to be able to hear many voices as they collaborated intentionally—those voices were trees. Trees are similar to our organization as they have chemicals identical to human neurotransmitters. Signals are created by ions cascading across fungal membranes (Simard, 2021, p.5).

Moreover, you are probably now asking what does a tree have to do with homo sapiens and storytelling? Great question you asked! She stated that during her research, she came upon one of her first clues about connectivity while tapping into the messages that the trees were relaying back and forth through a cryptic underground fungal network. When she followed the clandestine path of the conversations, she learned that this network is pervasive throughout the forest floor, connecting all the trees in a constellation of tree hubs and fungal links.

A crude map (oh, could this be an organizational hierarchy chart?) revealed that the biggest, oldest timers are the sources of fungal connections to regenerating seedlings. Not only that, but they also connect to all neighbors, young and old, serving as the linchpins for a jungle of threads and synapses and nodes. The most shocking aspect of this pattern is its similarities with the human brain. In it, the old and young perceive, communicate, and respond to one another by emitting chemical signals, chemicals identical to human neurotransmitters. Why do they have human-like behaviors, and why do they work like civil societies? The scientific evidence is impossible to ignore: the forest is wired for wisdom and healing (Simard, 2021, p. 6).

Embarking on a journey of wonder, just as our friends Campbell and Simard did, is a testament to how deeply human inquiry exists beyond data and technology; it is about understanding who we are and our places in the world. More of us should take walks through the forest and at least try to converse with a tree! When was the last time you talked to a tree? Another way to ask this may be, "What would inspire you along your journey to be a forest detective?"

From your curiosity, are you asking why the forest has human-like behaviors and why they work like civil societies? The scientific evidence is impossible to ignore: the forest is wired for wisdom and healing. In today's chaotic world, are our organizations wired for learning and healing? As a leader, you may want to embark on a journey of wonder beyond data and technology – and perhaps take walks through nature or dare to listen to a tree! When did you last listen to stories about the forest and the people in your organization? There is an organizational story to be told, find it and tell it!

This is a great place to bring in Powers (2018), who echoes the words of Campbell and Simard:

> That is the trouble with people, their root problem. Life runs alongside them, unseen. Right here, right next. Creating the soil. Cycling water. Trading in nutrients.

> Making weather. Building atmosphere. Feeding, curing, and sheltering more creatures than people can count. A chorus of living wood sings. If your mind were slightly greener, you would drown in meaning. The pine is saying something. There is something you need to hear. (p. 4)

Let me share a lived story

I was teaching a university graduate course where the students were police and fire department people. Their assignment was to wander into nature outside the classroom but on campus grounds and find a tree they felt connected to. They were to begin a conversation with that tree and write in their nature journals as they sat next to the tree, even leaning on the tree at times, what emotions they were feeling. They were also to name the tree, write about what they were hearing, and then think about how to take that emotional experience and appreciation for nature sounds into their workplaces. At first, the folks with the guns on their hips and the firefighters with their life-saving equipment hanging around their necks looked at me like I was a nut case who needed to be committed or, at the very least, given oxygen! However, they did not give up on me! After this experience, their demeanor was different when they re-entered the classroom. They walked differently and sounded different, and they even talked differently to each other. They asked about each other's trees, what they named them, and what the conversations were about.

This began the storytelling process, as they took these experiences into their workplaces to share with their colleagues. That would then lead to conversations about the fun and curiosity they experienced because of their nutty professor (yes, me!) and, of course, the sharing of what nature can teach them as they do their daily critical work.

From this classroom experience, the chief of police created a storytelling brown-bag luncheon to be held monthly so they could share stories. The dopamine was flowing! Dopamine is a substance that occurs naturally in the body. It improves the heart's pumping strength and blood flow to the kidneys. Aaah, the power of storytelling!

Eddie Woo echoes Suzanne Simard's words by introducing the concept of seeking out the patterns around us, including trees, lightning, and the Delfi River (2018). They all reveal similar patterns in storytelling. The vibe I hope you are getting here is that nature provides leaders with stories that connect, and sometimes, we humans need to work on the eloquent task of finding those stories. Remember that Suzanne Simard reminds us that nature gives us the gift of a whole new way to see the world of storytelling. I would encourage you to find that gift!

In their (1997) book, *Gung Ho*! Blanchard and Bowles teach leaders how to turn customers into full-fledged fans. They do this by introducing an inspirational story about business leaders who use the secret of Gung Ho – a technique to boost enthusiasm and performance and create astonishing results in the organization. The three cornerstones of Gung Ho are observed by watching:

- The Spirit of the Squirrel
- The Way of the Beaver
- The Gift of the Goose

If you are unfamiliar with their work, I encourage you to read *Gung Ho!* and share a copy with all your folks in the organization. Then, as the chief of police did, create brown bag sessions to share the learning through the story of animals—and their connection to humans!

Say Hello to Evelyn Clark

In Evelyn Clark's book, *Around the Corporate Campfire*, she states that wise leaders tell stories, and they periodically gather the *tribe* around the corporate campfire (the boardroom, annual meeting, holiday events, etc.) to recall the legends and share new tales (2004, p.ix). She shares a story told by Jim Sinegal, cofounder, President, and CEO of Costco Wholesale:

> What else do we have besides stories? Stories hit home with people and bring meaning to the work we do.

> A picture is worth a thousand words, and a story told appropriately is priceless. We describe one of our philosophies as stories. (p. xi)

Clark shared an analogy: A leader who can identify and develop an authentic corporate story and tell it effectively is similar to a masterful conductor who leads an orchestra through the most challenging musical arrangement. The storytelling leader can get everyone to play the same song, understand and identify corporate values, and enact them as part of their daily responsibilities (p. xii).

Let us meet Dr. Trent

A hard look at social and statistical narratives is informative, but we must continue from there, for they tell only one side of the story. In her book *The Awakened Woman*, Dr. Trent tells us that if we stay quiet, we become a statistic (2017, p. 105). When we collectively tell stories, there is a richness in that diversity that can create bold new futures, individually for ourselves and together as a human organization or a village, as Dr. Trent calls it (2017).

Storytelling is not something we sometimes do. It is the way we navigate the world minute by minute. A story is always running and evolving inside our heads, constructing reality about ourselves, others, and the world as we imagine it because the world is inherently a construct of our imaginations. You might ask yourself, "Do I have a bodacious imagination?"

Leaders, you can tell alternate, authentic, complex, messy stories, even your own stories. Unlike the usual, linear way to set goals, storytelling enables us to be imaginative and inspirational in those goals. When you tell a story to your organization, you allow others to revisit their stories to craft a new future creatively. Stories are little seeds we plant; who knows what will grow once they germinate? Some may not develop, but oh my, some will.

If an organization can imagine itself differently, the culture could live differently, too. Dr. Trent does not discuss storytelling as a form of therapy but rather as an act of creativity and creation. She speaks about telling stories as a mixture of knowing and mystery (2017). The organization should feel free of its current reality and stretch its boundaries. Through language, leaders can rewrite the stories, tell the stories as the protagonists, and tell the truth; otherwise, someone else will be measuring the organization's success—not those who inhabit it.

CHAPTER 11

THE WONDER FACTOR IN BEING THE STORYTELLER

Wonder is a feeling of curiosity and appreciation inspired by something beautiful, unfamiliar, or inexplicable. We tell stories in hopes of inciting that feeling. A passionately told story is contagious. For example, you may want to share the story where the firm's CEO plays a musical instrument, ties fishing flies, is a gourmet cook, does fine cabinetry, spends hours a week in a greenhouse, watches birds, or has some other craft that links them closely to the tangible world. Why, you ask? Because stories reflect our possibilities for transformation. Good leaders know that the question is not whether storytelling successfully communicates knowledge or can persuade individuals into action but rather whether the appropriate level of passion and the correct storytelling techniques can find ways to increase morale, imbue organizational ethos, and energize staff. A simple fable by Denning conveys a fictional story of a squirrel organization that, to be successful, needs to go from a nut-burying to a nut-storing organization. This action alone goes from improbability to an opportunity and can generate enthusiasm and teamwork, share critical knowledge, and ultimately lead the organization into a new era of significance. This simple squirrel analogy, told at the right time, can have a pivotal impact on the success or failure of any significant organizational effort (2004).

Storytelling is a craft that must be learned. Leaders spend a lifetime refining their art but only sometimes include the pursuit of wonder in their communications. Furthermore, until leaders realize they are the speakers in the 'emotional transportation business,' they may be unable to create a dynamic story in which people remember what was said. Speaking is a craft. However, we need to transport people to different emotions. Moreover, that is really what impacts people the most. Everybody has stories. People's souls have high adventures. This is the wonder factor that will move organizations; nothing else will. Campbell's view shows how stories and images are sacred things that are not static but kinetic, transformational in their capacity, and psychological in their perspective (1991).

The 'wonder' might sound frizzy. Do you ever wonder why middle managers become a statistic in the continuing middle management and senior professional blood bath? To stay on top of the fermenting global brew will require the pursuit of wonder. Work and business can be creative and exciting. A growth experience. A journey of lifelong learning and constant surprise. Brene' Brown tells us throughout her book *Atlas of the Heart* that wonder fuels our passion for exploration and learning, curiosity and adventure (2018). Researchers have found that we can lead people to cooperate, share resources, fully appreciate the value of others, and see themselves more accurately, evoking humility. Some researchers even believe that wonder-inducing events may be one of the fastest and most powerful personal change and growth methods. Furthermore, we do not need to stand on a cliff and see the Northern Lights to feel wonder. Sometimes, I think my dogs are staring into my soul, and at that moment in time, I feel a tremendous sense of wonder, and those moments take my breath away.

As organizational storytellers, I suspect that the story resonates with most of us with its small but grand revelations, especially in these topsy-turvy times. The best leaders understand what the folks who are the storytellers are trying to do. They are collaborators. They are out and about, nudging and cajoling, chatting, listening, and cheering. The ineffective leaders are wholesalers. They hide behind data, memos, and videotaped speeches to the masses. They do not connect or emote. For great leaders, each day is a fresh opportunity to experiment with a new approach with nothing less than a new persona. Who will you be today? How are you going to connect? Every day, the play begins anew.

Think of it this way . . .

Architecture is a visual art, and the buildings speak for themselves. Like an architect speaks through buildings, a storyteller speaks through stories. Architecture, as does a story, embodies a perfect blend of art and science. Stories are all around us. A puzzle-like approach is simply a tool for storytelling, in which one can see which pieces fit and where visually. Somewhat similar to the architect. Often, we come across people who are genuinely good at talking with an audience, but their stories still need to improve. You may have a good story; it just requires a little polishing to stand out and, probably more importantly, to be remembered. On most occasions, when people create data stories, they focus only on getting the correct characters and events that make the story, which does not guarantee a great story. While important, it is not enough. How these characters and events unfold in the story makes all the difference. A story leaves a mark when it can engage and enable the audience.

However, a single story is dangerous, as it is opposite the architect's building, which is seen as a single entity. The single-story creates stereotypes; the problem with stereotypes is not that they are untrue but incomplete. They make one story become the only story. When you, as the organizational storyteller, stretch the boundaries, be wary of the danger of a single story, as spoken to us by Chimamanda Ngozi Adichie in her 2009 TED Conference.

The Single Story

Chimamanda Adichie warns us that we risk a critical misunderstanding if we hear only a single story about another person or country (2009). The danger of creating a single story is that it repeatedly shows the people as one thing and only one thing and that is what they become. It is only possible to talk about a single story by talking about power. There is a word, an Igbo word, that relates to the power structures in the world, and that word is *nkali.* It is a noun that loosely translates to 'be greater than another.' Like the economic and political worlds, stories are defined by the principle of *nkali.* How they are told, who tells them, when they are told, and how many stories are told are dependent on power. Power is the ability to tell the story of another person or organization and make it the definitive story of that person and organization.

Our lives and our cultures are composed of many overlapping stories. She tells of how she found her authentic cultural voice and warns that we risk a critical misunderstanding if we hear only a single story about another person or country.

As Chimamanda tells us,

> "I thought about this when I left Nigeria to study in the United States. I was nineteen. My American roommate was shocked by me. She asked where I had learned to speak English so well and was confused when I said that Nigeria happened to have English as its official language. She asked if she could listen to what she called my "tribal music" and was consequently very disappointed when I produced my tape of Mariah Carey." (4.01 min)

She continues:

> "What struck me was this: She had felt sorry for me even before she saw me. Seeing me as an African, her default position toward me was a patronizing, well-meaning

> pity. My roommate had a single story of Africa: a single story of catastrophe. In this single story, there was no possibility of Africans being similar to her, no possibility of feelings more complex than pity, and no possibility of a connection as human equals." (4.37 min)

We learn from her that if you create a single story as the organizational storyteller, you risk repeatedly showing people as one thing, as only one thing, and that is what they become.

CHAPTER 12

DO NOT FEAR THE DRAMATURG

There is a need to demystify the storytelling process because it is somewhat mysterious. We might ask, "Why is it so difficult?" The answer is partly because we need to remember that stories are much more about the audience than about the characters and the plot and much more critical than the storyteller. It takes tremendous courage to put your soul on paper and have people who are probably much less talented than you, certainly much less creative than you, trample all over the story. Remember, however, that those who judge have not yet figured out that tarmacs and paved roads harden the heart and soften the brain.

Be the leader who adds their voice to the telling; be part of the continuum of storytelling that often has no beginning or end.

A storyteller is nothing without the ability to inspire the listener to embody the tale's experience and invoke action; practice being a storyteller with the organizational vision firmly in your mind.

Dr. Trent explains it this way (2017):

- First, practice telling yourself the story with confidence.
- Then set an intention that you will be bold enough this week to tell someone else.

- Identify a safe person or group with whom you can share the story.
- It may be a person you do not know initially because the interpersonal distance is comforting.
- Protect yourself by avoiding telling family members or friends who may have their reasons for doubting you.
- Cultivate your *tinogona spirit. Your tinogona spirit is your inner resilience,* driven by determination gracefully and compassionately, knowing you can achieve anything.
- Okay, this part might seem weird but tell the story so you feel the words take shape in your mouth and hang in the air.

Do Not Fear the Dramaturg

Any veteran storyteller will agree that there is no substitute for practicing. Getting the story right is critical, as much for motivating ourselves as for enlisting the help of others. Anyone trying to make a change has to work out a story that connects the old and the new. We often fail in a transition period, yet most need to link our past, present, and future into a compelling whole.

One of the storyteller's primary roles is not misusing the stories. Stories are not ads, sermons, lectures, or doctrines. Do not try to hijack the storytelling by using your tale to solicit agreement from the listeners. Instead, include the little pieces of your story that spice up everyone's conversations in a frame within which all followers can make sense of their places in the organization. Remember, as you lead through storytelling, with the simplest of elements, you create a vivid verbal tapestry in the followers' minds.

The risk, however, is that over-dramatization slows storytelling down to the extent that the bond between the audience and teller is broken, and the story ceases to function. There are differences between theater and storytelling; theater is not "real" somewhere because that journey is not absolute; it is pretending. As the leader, do not walk across empty spaces because they are not going anywhere; you have arrived and have a story to tell. Be real. Make the transition with your storytelling by keeping your integrity intact. Yes, there is a danger in the first-person voyage through the storytelling of seeming merely ludicrous. However, what if that is precisely what the story itself requires?

So, what is a dramaturg? A dramaturg is a member of a production's artistic team who specializes in transforming a script into a meaningful living performance (Chemers, 2023). Mark Bly, former chair of the Dramaturgy and Playwriting Program at Yale University, comes as close as anyone ever explaining the function of the dramaturg, which, as he stated, is the very blood cursing through the veins of a theatrical production (Chemers, 2023, p.1). In practice, dramaturgy refers to the accumulated techniques that all theatrical artists employ to do three things (Chemers, 2023, p.5):

1. Determine the aesthetic architecture of a piece of dramatic literature (analysis).
2. Discover everything needed to transform the inert script into a living theater piece (research).
3. Apply that knowledge in a way that makes sense to a living audience at this time and place (practical application).

Do not fear *dramaturg*, the term used for those responsible for ensuring integrity in storytelling. The dramaturg revels in telling you that you are full of hokey nonsense. Keeping things in perspective is quite tricky. The difficulty is directly proportional to the heap size you are sitting atop. Somehow, you have to stay in touch with reality. A dramaturg is a person who can laugh at you. More than that, the dramaturg makes you laugh at yourself. When Roman senators addressed the masses, they had a group of underlings behind them whose whole job was to lean over and repeat, remember, you are mortal. You are, too, and had best be reminded of it often and bluntly.

Whether you are a seasoned leader or just entering that adventure, use the dramaturg who comes with fresh eyes, is a critical observer, and will identify the ambiguities and help you clarify plots in the stories you are telling or wish to speak. It would be best to have these dramaturgs, as they will ask you pragmatically what the audience will get from your story. Dramaturgy plays a central role in the creative development of your stories, making the best use of your combined skills and energies. Often, leaders have certain mannerisms within their working methods, which are now blocks. Letting go of old habits and learning to trust the story is a great creative and innovative liberation for the leader.

Oh, but wait, do not dismiss the dramaturg after the storytelling event has ended, as you need to gain an awareness of what worked, the audience's reaction, and their perceptions. This reflective conversation with the dramaturg will release the hitherto untapped potential and life in your storytelling and may increase your confidence to take more creative risks.

Show no fear, or okay, a slight sense of nervousness when your dramaturg brings humor into your storytelling preparation. In their book *Humor, Seriously: Why Humor is a Secret Weapon in Business and Life*, Jennifer Aaker and Naomi Bagdonas wrote that anyone can harness humor, even you (2021).

The law of fun is allowed to supersede the law of gravity. If we think differently than this way when prepping and delivering stories, the experiences we may need to remember that appropriate humor has the potential to transform work and life.

I set out to look at both. I use the word *appropriate. Knowing what people find funny, suitable,* and relevant is far from universal, and no one nails it every time. Ask your dramaturg to give you tools to recognize your gaffes, diagnose your storytelling situation, and make it right when you accidentally cross a line. By understanding the psychological science, mechanics, and applications of humor in storytelling, we can shift how we look at the world and how it looks back at us.

Your dramaturg is the crucial person who can work with you through this debunking exercise, but only if you let them. Once again, do not fear the dramaturg. Remember that storytelling plays close to the big fire, which is the truth. The listeners feel the heat.

CHAPTER 13

THE HUMOR INGREDIENT

The collective loss of a sense of humor is a serious problem afflicting people and organizations globally, which is understandable in today's environment. We seem to be going over the humor cliff, tumbling down into the abyss of solemnity. According to numerous research studies, at the bottom of this abyss is where the frequency at which we laugh or smile each day starts to plummet. To some extent, this pattern makes sense. Before we go over the cliff, as adults in the workforce, we become profound and influential people, trading laughter for ties and suits. Is this you? Be honest here.

Do we lose fun in a sea of the bottom line, slide decks, and mind-numbing conference calls? Do you hear a collective yawn? Our sense of joy is repressed by a dizzyingly complex and dynamic professional environment, full of social landmines that are difficult to gauge and feel safe to avoid. As a result, most of us keep our interactions sterile, measured, and professional; we go to work each day and leave our sense of humor and so much more of ourselves at the door. This response signals a fundamental misunderstanding about how to work, how to solve critical significant problems, how to conduct ourselves, and how to be successful. We do not need more professionalism in the workplace. Instead, we need more of ourselves and more human connections, especially as video chats and more relationships replace in-person meetings sustained entirely by social media. What is holding us back? The global pandemic would be a valid answer. However, is that an excuse that will last into the future?

Four themes may need debunking. Our choosing, right? Aaker and Bagdonas identify those four themes (2021).

- Humor has no place amid serious work.
- There is a deep, paralyzing fear that the storyteller's humor will fail.
- To use humor and fun in the workplace, one must be funny.
- Many people believe that humor is an innate ability, not a skill you can learn.

Because of humor's role in relationship dynamics, storytelling with humor is a fundamentally communicative process. It is embedded within a message sent by an individual with particular motivations to a receiver who must interpret that use of humor within an organizational context. A skillful spirit facilitates communicative goals and creates a space where meaning is shared and trust is earned. Humor is in many research fields, like psychology, philosophy, linguistics, and sociology, not just in the business world.

In line with this idea, Cheng and Wang (2014) hypothesized that humor may provide a respite from tedious situations in the workplace. This *mental break* prevents work-related depletion and facilitates the replenishment of cognitive resources, ultimately allowing people to persist longer on complex tasks.

In today's corporate world, there is a mistaken belief that we must always be serious to be taken seriously. However, the research tells a different story: humor can be one of our most powerful tools for accomplishing severe things. Research shows that humor makes us appear more competent and confident, strengthens relationships, unlocks creativity, and boosts resilience during difficult times. The global pandemic is a perfect example. In addition, humor fends off a permanent and unsightly frown known as the *resting boss face* (Aaker & Bagdonas, 2021). For those who intuitively understand humor's power, few know how to wield it with intention. As a result, humor is vastly underleveraged in most workplaces today, impacting individual performance, relationships, and organizational health.

President Eisenhower once said, "A sense of humor is part of the art of leadership, getting along with people, and getting things done " (Smith, 2022, para 2). If President Eisenhower, the second least naturally funny president ever (after Franklin Pierce), thought humor was necessary to win wars, build highways, and warn against the military-industrial complex, then as leaders, you may consider learning it, too.

People are drawn to storytelling in various settings for many reasons today. We learn to communicate through metaphor and image at a very young age. Storytelling is a common language, however extreme or surprising it may be. Stories are the moral and imaginative frame of life, including organizational life. A sense of profound connection comes through in a story. The stories we keep in our heads and hearts are the maps that allow us to understand the stream of events that make up our lives. All human and animal life, even trees and flowers, comes with a storytelling lineage. Every organization has its unique sayings and expressions. As a leader, this is the culture in which you create.

In his book *The Humor Advantage: Why Some Businesses are Laughing All the Way to the Bank* (2013), Kerr discusses how the amount or type of humor in any workplace depends almost entirely on the culture. He discusses how humor can drive creativity and innovation at work, how humor lowers stress at work, how humor can help brand your business to attract customers, and how humor can help you turn your long-term customers into passionate fans.

Humor plays a vital role in enhancing creativity and innovation at work. It creates a relaxed environment where employees feel comfortable sharing ideas, encourages out-of-the-box thinking, and boosts collaboration. Humor also lowers stress by lightening the mood, reducing tension, and fostering resilience, which helps employees manage pressure more effectively.

For businesses, humor is a powerful branding tool. A lighthearted approach can make a company more relatable and appealing to customers, setting it apart from competitors. It humanizes the brand, making it easier to connect with and attract new clients. Additionally, humor helps transform long-term customers into passionate fans by creating memorable experiences. These positive associations strengthen customer loyalty, fostering a deeper emotional connection with the brand.

CHAPTER 14

BE THE GAME CHANGER

Using courage and passion to tell stories can be game-changing. To make sense of the layers of events that occur in interactions with others, we organize everything that happens to us into coherent stories. Our stories are formed in constant dialogue with events and people and tell us how we perceive the circumstances, the people around us, and ourselves with the experiences.

Experiences, anecdotes, and case studies provide evidence of a relational construct characterized by one's ability to establish and nurture respect and trust among people, in addition to being flexible and resilient. However, let us not kid ourselves: language and power are inextricably linked. The spoken word pushes thoughts out of someone's head and into the open. This is often difficult, as it is often a battle. However, it can be won through storytelling. Experiences, when packed in a story framework, become that catalyst to uncover the unsaid words that, if they remain inside us, allow the toxicity to mainstay.

Begin to use stories and then watch the magic happen. This will help others see the connections, understand how the pieces fit, and not be fearful but welcome a mighty future.

Storytelling never begins in a box but rather constantly explores new ways of thinking and working fueled by dramatic changes in the world.

These changes include rapid technological advances, changing notions about work, new markets and sources of competition, the impact of new business arrangements, and the global pandemic the world has experienced.

We are living through a time of unprecedented and troubling change. We have come to a crossroads where old and familiar customs have broken down, but the new oral frame and social structure are still evolving. We enter the future less connected to ancestral guidance than any human generation before us. Although we have invented remarkable data-saving technologies, we must remember the stories. We broadcast our voices over vast distances but talk less to those around us.

Writing a book about oral art is a contradiction and a very old one. When Socrates took his famous walk with Phaedrus outside the gates of Athens, he told the story about the time in Egypt when the inventor God Theuth came to King Thamus to show off his latest improved time-saving invention: a tool for memory and wisdom. He called it *writing*. King Thamus warned Theuth that if men learn this, it will implant forgetfulness in their souls; they would cease to exercise memory because they would rely on what is written, calling things to remembrance no longer from within but using external marks. What a fabulous conversation that would have been to hear!

Donald Davis (2014), an American storyteller, explained in his TEDx Charlottesville to an audience, "As a storyteller, I only give you the words. How you hear those words turns them into a story." This is listening with a mind to remember, where listeners know that one day, they may pass the fable on when it is their turn. In other words, the story speaks only when you can lend your voice through the narrative. In delivering communication, there is no division between style and content. Leaders are both style and content. Listeners do not get a carton of content and a dollop of style. They bring a cocktail where style and content are all mixed.

Denning (2011) describes the storytelling cocktail this way:

- The most important is eye contact.
- The second element follows from the first: throw away your notes. You cannot make eye contact if you are reading from notes.

- Next, get out from behind any podium between you and the audience. Podiums block the flow of psychic energy.
- Then make sure you maintain an open body stance, square shoulders, relaxed, calm, assertive, with a total focus on the audience. If you are there for them, they will be there for you.
- Make sure your gestures are in sync with the content of what you are saying. Gestures serve as a kind of visual punctuation to the words. They should reflect contagious energy and enthusiasm. Finally, face the audience squarely and openly. If necessary, wiggle your toes to remind yourself not to perambulate, which is massively distracting. Do not walk from side to side across the speaker's platform. He says that if these elements sound mundane, even trivial, the difference between someone respecting simple principles and someone is not stark.

Leaders need to communicate in a way that fits human beings' thinking. It mirrors the peculiarities of the human mind and heart. As a result, people can see possibilities that were hitherto invisible to them. As these new possibilities open up, the listeners are willing to assist with reimagining and recreating the future. This is the significance of the narrative: the storyteller should be so engaged with the story that the listeners become drawn into the narrative's world.

When exploring their book *Gamestorming,* Gray et al. (2010), we learn that a story is similar to a game. It evolves in stages: imagine the world, create the world, open the world, explore the world, and then close the world.

> *Imagine the world*: Before the story begins, you must imagine a world where everyone can explore ideas or possibilities.
>
> *Create the world*: A story is formed by giving it boundaries and artifacts. Boundaries are the spatial and temporal boundaries of the world, such as the culture or geographical landscape. Artifacts are carriers of

meaning; for example, writing an idea on a sticky note creates an information artifact.

Open the world: A story can only work if what the story represents is authentic to the listeners.

Explore the world: Values and goals are the forces that drive exploration.

Close the world: A story is completed when its purpose has been met. Although the storyteller may feel gratification and accomplishment, did the audience feel connected to the story and thus become emotionally engaged as listeners?

Suppose you, as the organizational storyteller, can create the space for folks to explore and examine challenges and generate novel insights about how their world works. In that case, there may be awe-inspiring possibilities to find. You have within you the storytelling power to do so by opening the vast world to breakthrough thinking and innovation.

Embarking on an exploration of challenges is akin to a voyage of discovery. Like Columbus, you may begin your journey by searching for a route to India, but you might find something like America: completely different, but perhaps more valuable.

In storytelling, fire-starting techniques are the sparks that ignite the imagination and call for adventure. They initiate a quest or search. How you start the fire is essential in the wilderness; the same is true in storytelling. Start a story or a fire in the wrong way or place, and you may find things getting out of control.

Not everything comes to you in order at the beginning of developing your storyteller's craft. It is rumored that William S. Burroughs determined the order of his book *Naked Lunch* (1962) by throwing the manuscript in the air and assembling the pages in the order he picked them up. Often, we seek and find patterns everywhere we look. I often thought about using Burroughs' technique when writing this book, and his technique just possibly have been used throughout these pages.

CHAPTER 15

WE ARE ALL CHARACTERS IN EACH OTHER'S STORIES

Leaders who tell stories compellingly communicate essential messages in memorable ways, develop more effective relationships with those they lead, and create inspirational culture as their organizations go through turmoil. Storytelling does not need to be a foreign concept, as we can all search our histories and experiences for important lessons learned that can be communicated as a narrative. Storytelling contributes to a positive organizational approach—fostering positive organizational psychology and an environment where everyone feels they belong, possibly a fun workplace.

We are all characters in each other's stories. If we could see all our stories in their real-life fullness, we would discover they all intersect. Through stories, we can vividly experience our interconnectedness and the incredibly complex web of mutual relationships that is the universe.

Stories are more than dramas people tell or read. As a pattern, stories are a powerful way for an organization to explore and co-create shared realities. Our psyches and cultures are filled with narrative fields of influence, or *story fields*, which shape the awareness and behavior of individuals and collectives associated with them.

The reality is that we recognize that every person, every being, and everything has a story and contains stories. We are surrounded by stories, embedded in stories, and made of stories – even our birth is a story. Everything that exists has, embodies, and participates in many lived stories. A number by itself means nothing. With the gaining significance of data communications, Sejal Vora (2019) stated that every business aspect that deals with data needs a story to make the dry facts and figures more interesting, engaging, and impactful. According to Vora (2019), we need to understand the four-dimensional impacts that narratives make and which data does not.

1. Data is boring; stories make it enjoyable.
2. Data is complex, and stories facilitate understanding.
3. Data does not command action—stories do.
4. Data is forgotten; stories leave impressions.

The storyteller is always collecting ideas, words, phrases, and stories. Only some of them are destined for a leader's repertoire. The rest are equally valuable, although you may never tell them publicly within your organization. The stories you tell will inform your moral philosophy, tune your tongue and ear, and help stretch your imagination. Storytellers discover narrative material from a wide range of wellsprings. It is a matter of walking through life with open ears and a story-seeking soul. Listen to the wind in the trees. If leaders look, they find reverence in nature. Isn't that what Simard told us in her book 2021, *Finding the Mother Tree*?

One of the first things that will catch your attention as a storyteller is the sheer originality of spoken language in everyday life. You will hear delicious turns of phrase, hilarious slips of the tongue, and wonderfully imaginative words of mouth everywhere. For example, "they taste like shoes and smell like socks" describes mushroom-flavored risotto.

As you develop your storytelling art, collect phrases with all the joy of a gem collector finding a new ruby or emerald. Then, demonstrate how much spontaneity and creativity can be seen in daily conversations. Sometimes, the phrases do wind up in a story. This does take listening – so brush up on that skill if needed!

As storytellers, we understand that the value of a story lies not just in its content but in the diverse and engaging ways it is told. Your voice and the language of your story must captivate the listener's ear as thoroughly as a sonata, a jazz riff, a gospel song, or a piece of hip-hop. If all the languages in your story sounded the same, how would the listener's ear distinguish between the most significant moment and the casual throw-away line? Here, you would hear a collective yawn in our audience.

CHAPTER 16

BE THE STEWARD

Being the steward of your organization is a profoundly simple idea. Growing a business and developing leaders takes a courageous and innovative leader. For example, as the leader, have you thought about how the creative juices flow when folks draw or doodle pictures, go on treasure hunts, take things apart, test the physical properties of a Slinky, play catch, explore, question, and have fun? It sounds like a winning business strategy that will generate successful new products and services—an entirely new way of doing business!

Enter the Chief Imagination Officer (CIO), whose role is to create an entirely different mindset and conversation inside organizations. An example is Ted Waitt, a co-founder of Gateway, a five-billion-dollar computer supplier that ships its cow-spotted boxes around the globe and has an official role in the company's imagination. Hopefully, this piques your curiosity about the need for a chief imagination officer—or possibly you already know your organization needs a Chief Imagination Officer.

What skills are required to be a CIO? A CIO can imagine, reimagine, and craft outcomes from opportunities. Consider Leo Li, who was previously a CIO at Apple until he became the chairman of the Global Semiconductor Alliance. He is a well-known and respected figure in the semiconductor industry (2018). He helped grow the revenue at

Spreadtrum from $100 million to $2 billion and increased the company's market value from $35 million to $7.5 billion. This kind of growth and success is the potential a CIO can unlock in a company (Farrell, 2018).

Suppose storytelling has become the big business, science, and brand marketing communications nom du jour - then curiosity is essential for keeping companies at least one step ahead of their competitors. Unfortunately, many companies work hard to reinforce their sets of particular guidelines and suck the creativity out of people.

As leaders and followers, we should be curious about what our customers need and how their needs are changing; how a world of remarkable new technologies can be applied and delivered; what the new workforce wants from employers; and what will enthuse and energize people to spend most of their waking hours in an organization.

One way is for leaders to commit to wandering around, smelling the flowers, and picking up the snails on the way. Simard would remind you to spend an afternoon walking through the woods to find clues to your company's success. What would the natural world and its other inhabitants think about the problems or opportunities you may be wrestling with? Maybe make time to befriend snails and other creatures to learn their mysteries. Leaders need to be open to 'new.'

You may throw your arms up and say, "This is all nice, but how does the leader responsible for the unit's bottom-line success infuse such curiosity into the company?" Before you do that, ask yourself if there will even be a company if you do not.

Noel Tichy wrote in *The Leadership Engine* that the best way to get humans to venture into unknown terrain is to make that terrain familiar and desirable by taking them there first in their imaginations (2007). *Aha!* I thought. Here is a place where storytelling, perhaps the most potent route to people's imaginations, could prove indispensable.

Luhn posits that the feeling is the message (2018). You must be vulnerable and honest to create authentic stories and exercise restraint when delivering your message. Be sentimental, not saccharine. Future leaders rise to prominence fueled by well-honed skill sets, only to falter when they do not use the courage to be the storytellers who then fuel the organizational tank of energy and enthusiasm and express the willingness to take on the roles of the informal leaders who share cultural stories throughout the organization.

Campbell told us that we recover the treasures of life by going down into the abyss. Where we stumble, there lies our treasure (2008). In my humble opinion about leadership, the foundation of our greatness is telling stories where the glory can be found.

This is an excellent place to introduce the C2 factor, curiosity, and courage to help leaders become champions. Author Joanne Irving suggests leaders may risk becoming robotic when the landscape shifts (2022). An approach to preventing that from happening is to become organizational storytellers who effectively blend a lion's courage with a cat's curiosity. You need not be slaying dragons in the organization to be that leader. In these challenging moments, we must stay curious and resist choosing comfort over courage. It is brave to invite new information to the table, sit with it, and hear it out, which is rare nowadays. A practice Irving encourages is to ideate through brainstorming, which is the roadmap to becoming an organizational storyteller (2022). Tom Peters reminds us that brainstorming is not about looking for answers. There are no answers, just many questions that need to be asked and, at best, a few guesses at answers that might be worth trying (1994).

However, whatever methodology a leader uses to encourage openness and reduce fear so that people can be authentic, the degree of dialog occurring without prejudging them is the stepping stone for everyone in the organization to be storytellers—not just leaders who have the title of leader, but everyone. That, my friends, is how grassroots cultures become the workplace fabric.

Speaking of cultures, Brown's book *Atlas of the Heart* (2022) maps meaningful connections as we have the grounded confidence to both tell our stories and be the stewards of the stories that we hear. Brown connects to Irving as they both express that wonder fuels our passion for exploration and learning, curiosity and adventure, and awe. Researchers often write that awe-inducing events may be one of the fastest and most powerful methods of leader growth and organizational change.

So, what is the connection? It is the energy between people when they feel seen, heard, and valued; when they give and receive without judgment; and then they derive sustenance and strength from the relationship.

Go ahead, leaders; look in your leadership mirror. Do you exhibit connection throughout your organization?

Chief Storyteller is such a foreign job title. However, Denver and Atlanta have followed Detroit's lead and hired their storytellers to help spruce up the metro areas' images and engage with residents by producing stories about unique people and places or local history that the mainstream media has ignored. Aaron Foley, a local journalist, expected blank stares, questions, and doubts when he officially became the City of Detroit's chief storyteller in 2016. Raju Narisetti, a journalism professor at Columbia University, sees parallels with the 18th-century town criers, who delivered news and information directly to neighborhoods. Others see a prototype in Humans of New York, a photography project documenting the Big Apple's street people that has evolved into a worldwide urban storytelling phenomenon (Williams, 2019).

The narrative detail, often at the heart of a good story, is one of the most potent forms of communication. Indeed, storytelling has enjoyed a renaissance, with storytelling-based approaches being used in everything from promoting new startups to inspiring creativity in the workplace to mapping business leadership strategy – and, yes, urban storytelling. This is because stories, particularly organizational stories, can illuminate fault lines, highlight oddities, and paint pictures of the past, present, and future that are compelling and easily understandable.

The science community has also started to embrace the power of storytelling, as illustrated by the popularity of science storytelling organizations such as *The Story Collider*, science storytelling socials at the Annual Society for Neuroscience (SFN) meeting, and SFN mini-symposia devoted to the topic of storytelling (https://www.storycollider.org/).

Engaging listeners in the scientific journey creates a more robust, meaningful knowledge transfer. It elicits participation and creates an intellectual investment and emotional bond between the speaker and the audience.

Professor Hasson:

> I have always used storytelling to communicate science to my colleagues because the backstory behind how a scientific question gets answered is as interesting as the data generated. Engaging listeners in the scientific journey creates a more substantial, more meaningful knowledge transfer. It causes participation and creates an intellectual investment and emotional bond between the speaker and the audience (https://www.storycollider.org/).

Dr. Feliú-Mójer:

> I combine storytelling with my scientific and cultural backgrounds to make science more accessible and inclusive to communities that are underrepresented in and excluded from science. For example, I co-produced a series called "Background to Breakthrough" that flips the narrative about the value of diversity in science (https://www.storycollider.org/).

This is an excellent place to introduce *Humanocracy*, authored by Gary Hamel and Michele Zanini (2020). They draw on more than a decade of research to create a detailed blueprint for creating organizations as inspired and ingenious as the human beings inside them. They identified five critical building blocks, to which I now add storytelling as the sixth building block. Right now, you are probably asking, "What is humanocracy?"

Simply stated, humanocracy is to think like an activist. You can make a decisive contribution to enriching your colleagues' lives and helping your organization flourish in a world that, however unsettling, is awash in opportunity. Leaders must not flinch or look away but instead confront what we have long known: our organizations are hindered by their inhumanity.

The question at the heart of humanocracy is what sort of organization elicits and merits the best human beings can give? The implication of storytelling in this shift in perspective is profound. We must rid ourselves of bureaucratic mindsets, rethink our core assumptions about leading, and know that in humanocracy, the organization is the instrument. It is the vehicle human beings use to serve the organization better.

How does storytelling come into play here?

Most of us would have been reluctant to sail with Columbus, and many are probably hesitant to embark on the journey to humanocracy. While data and courage may get your colleagues to the port, most will hesitate to step aboard - unless you can paint a picture of the destination. Luckily, this is where your organizational storytelling talent comes in – paint the destination through a story.

Another way to converse about humanocracy is by Dr. Trent, who told us that our stories have magic—they give shape and purpose (2017). Storytelling has depth that brings collective empathy, reminding us of the essence of our humanity, the *ubuntu*, the humanness that makes us human beings.

CHAPTER 17

STORYTELLING IS BIG BUSINESS

In exploring the material for this book, I looked at not only the scientific research behind the power of storytelling but also considered how to master a specific set of concepts from the world of storytelling and its impact on the bottom line of a business. Storytelling is not a panacea for necessary programs, strategies, or budgets; it is a tool that can assist in facilitating the vision and mission of the organization. Whether we are leading in corporate settings, academic organizations, neighborhoods, or on a global scale, leaders must constantly challenge themselves to be a yardstick of resilience. Take a moment and re-read Leo Li in the previous chapter and how he impacted the bottom line - he helped grow the revenue at Spreadtrum from $100 million to $2 billion. He increased the company's market value from $35 million to $7.5 billion.

In his book *Powerful Times* (2005), Eamonn Kelly describes how we are not in an age of change but in a shift of ages. He described this point in history as the most significant period of social change since the Renaissance. From a view looking backward into Greek philosophy, Heraclitus believed that the universe was characterized by constant change. In the change process, he provoked questions about the reality of change and those who led the change. Even Plato accounted for change and stability by assigning them different realms. If we fast forward to today, and even though storytellers may stumble and tumble as they learn their craft, it is desperately necessary to lead from this approach in a mind-boggling nutty world.

Consider research done by the Forum Corporation, which analyzes commercial customers. This research revealed that 70 percent of lost customers hit the road not because of price or quality issues but because they did not like the human side of doing business with the prior product or service provider (Peterson, 2017). In the age of e-mail, social media, supercomputer power on our phones, and the raucous global village, attentiveness, a token of human connectedness, is the greatest gift we can give someone. This is achievable through authentic storytelling. Through story listening, we gain new perspectives and better understand the world. We challenge and expand our understanding by exploring how others see and understand the world through their lens.

A leader's responsibility is to transform people's ideas and notions about their businesses into a narrative form that helps build the brand and clarifies their journey for employees. If everyone in the organization understands the story of who they collectively are, it can help employees pull together and create greatness. Stories tell us who we are and what we think we are doing. Applied to a business, this can be incredibly powerful.

Denning (2011) was once asked if stories have a role in business. He answered yes. Analysis might excite the mind, but it hardly offers a route to the heart. At a time when corporate survival often requires transformational change, leadership involves inspiring people to act in unfamiliar and frequently unwelcome ways. Mind-numbing cascades of numbers or daze-inducing PowerPoint slides will not achieve this goal. Even logical arguments for making the needed changes usually will not do the trick. However, compelling storytelling often does. In fact, in certain situations, nothing else works.

Storytelling has become the big business, science, and brand marketing communications *nom du jour*. Periodicals and journals from Forbes to Business Week, Parents Journal, Discover, and Science are peppered with recent articles touting storytelling's value, power, and effectiveness. Storytelling has the power to alter beliefs, values, and behaviors. It exerts a powerful influence. Nevertheless, only a tiny fraction of all the 'stories' we hear or read accomplish that herculean feat. Hopefully, you are asking why only 88% to 90% of all the stories we hear or read do not affect us. One reason is that they are not vividly imagined in our minds. Alternatively, they do not engage us deeply emotionally; thus, they are not remembered, possibly because we do not learn from them as they are told.

The mind is deeply emotional. It tells the organizational story! Take the organization's data and turn it into real people doing real things, and you might impact the direction the organization wishes to head toward. Leaders who tell stories compellingly, memorably communicate essential messages, develop more effective relationships with those they lead, and create an inspirational culture as their organizations go through turmoil, such as the recent global pandemic. Storytelling can be something other than a foreign concept, as we can all search our history and experiences for lessons learned that can be communicated through a narrative. Storytelling contributes to an optimistic organizational approach – positive in the sense of positive organizational psychology, an environment where everyone feels they belong.

CHAPTER 18

THE ART OF VOICE

The power of storytelling lies in the words we choose and how we give them life. In every great story, the art of voice serves as the heartbeat, infusing characters, scenes, and emotions with depth and resonance. Voice is the invisible thread that draws listeners and readers into the world of the narrative, transforming simple words on a page into vivid, emotional experiences. Whether spoken aloud or written, it carries the storyteller's unique style, mood, and perspective, making each tale distinct and memorable.

Throughout history, master storytellers have harnessed the art of voice to create powerful connections with their audiences. Take Maya Angelou, for instance, whose rich, lyrical voice in her spoken performances and writings created an unmistakable presence. Her autobiographical works, such as *I Know Why the Caged Bird Sings* (2009), echoed her rhythm and tone, conveying strength and vulnerability in equal measure. Angelou's voice was more than just her words—it embodied her experiences, heritage, and worldview.

Similarly, in fiction, writers like García and Garcia (2016) captured the essence of their culture through voices imbued with magical realism. Their distinct storytelling, with its fluid blend of the real and the fantastical, created a world where the lines between truth and myth blurred. Voice was not just a style but a portal, pulling readers into the depths of Latin American life and imagination.

Oral storytellers, too, have used their voices to captivate and inspire. For example, the griots of West Africa have passed down history, culture, and values through generations using rhythm, intonation, and song. Their vocal expressions were not merely tools for entertainment but vital cultural bridges, keeping history alive through spoken word. The way they tell stories is inseparable from their identity as oral historians.

In modern times, the influence of voice in storytelling continues with figures like David Attenborough, whose calm and authoritative narration has shaped how we experience nature documentaries. His unique voice has become synonymous with the natural world, guiding viewers through facts and an emotional connection to the planet.

These storytellers, among countless others, have shown us that voice is more than just a delivery mechanism—it is the story's soul. By examining literary and oral traditions, we can better understand how voice breathes life into stories, turning them into lasting legacies.

Let us meet a few of those storytellers through their voices

Alice Kane

Once upon a time, there was a storyteller, Alice Kane (1995). People sometimes passed her in the street and sat beside her in the streetcar, thinking she was much like any other woman – and she was, but she was not. It was not just the words she spoke in a story; other people often used them. It was how she said them. Moreover, the way she told them came from what she saw.

You may want to study her delivery methods to enhance your art of voice; in other words, are you crisp, nondramatic, full of little rising tones, like lapping water, and confident knowing that your voice can bandage the entire broken organization – or the world as Kane would say. Kane was once asked, as she sat frail in her wheelchair, what the master words of a great storyteller are. What is the master word that can communicate a legacy of stories, a technique for telling them, and the joy of language spoken so unforgettably? However, of course, with storytelling, there is no 'master word,' only the story, connecting people in a fragile thread or chain of narrative, always at risk of breaking and always needing the storyteller's powers of remembrance.

In an oral culture, a story is heard; in some who listen, it becomes a vision. Those of its hearers who learn to see the story can tell it later themselves. Those who do not may learn to summarize or recite it, but that differs from telling the story. Alice sees what she means and reveals what she sees. Often, she has not only images, events, and names of characters but also turns of phrase from a book; nevertheless, she tells the story instead of reciting the text. She may tell the same tale dozens of times and insist that she is telling it the same way, in the exact words, every time – yet each telling is different because each telling grows afresh from the vision.

Alice Kane's achievements and legacy are more significant because she practiced her art with steadiness and grace. She made herself an elder of the tribeless and the tribe. If we substitute the word tribe for organization, what will your legacy be?

Alice would turn to Dr. Trent and introduce her as a storyteller who tells a lived story, planted her dreams in the earth, and inspired them to grow – yes, through her voice. She reminds us that the importance of stories awakens the silent voice that may remain in us.

Dr. Alan Gregerman

Encouraging wonder should include challenging us to use our imaginations and think differently. It means asking people to look at the world around them for new ideas and inspirations that can be translated into tangible improvements in how we do business. Gregerman (2000) asks us to rediscover what can and should inspire us:

- New
- Difficult to figure out

- Cool to us
- Cool to someone whose opinion we value
- Found in nature (Simard would agree!)

Just for fun and profit, Gregerman lists some things we can do today to rediscover the gift of imagination and wonder to improve the bottom-line success (p. 122); one example is:

Visit a Museum: Spend a day at a museum of your choice, getting ideas for improving an area of your business. Find things in the museum that make you wonder and imagine possibilities for enhancing your business performance.

Let me share a story told by Gregerman:

> Rubbermaid executives were meeting in London. They decided to visit the British Museum, which houses one of the world's significant collections of antiquities and culture. Their assignment was simple: to look closely at how people lived in other civilizations and eras, with an eye toward the activities Rubbermaid products intended to serve. Not only was this act of curiosity stimulating, but it also resulted in several new and improved products. (p. 117).

Robert Fulgham

Fulgham (1991) shares a lived story that conjures up an image that may stay with you for a while:

> When turning to leave the grocery store, I was confronted with a sign. The automatic doors were broken. The sign said: Please Note – The Only Way Out is IN. As always, how one perceives the door determines the coming and going. One must make two journeys to have balance – OUT there and IN here. One depends upon the other. Every exit is an

> entrance. The door swings both ways. One must turn to resources within to move out in the world. (p. 92)

Fulgham introduces us to Dr. Brewster Higley, who, despite the hardships of his life, found time to sit on a stump in the sunshine – in front of his cabin in the silence of that place – and write stories. One of his stories was found by a patient, who read it aloud and urged the doctor to get it set to music. Doc Higley took the patient's advice and carried the story to Smith Center, Kansas, to share with his friend, the local pharmacist. Kelly had been a bugler in the Civil War, played several other musical instruments, and liked to compose songs. He was joined one night by several of his friends, and soon, a song was born from Higley's story. The song is "Home on the Range," which you would probably sing because if there is one song you likely know by heart, this is it.

People who have never seen Kansas, buffalo, deer, or antelope can sing this song. The story is summarized in the spirit of that song.

Aaah, once again, the power of a story!

Rob Biesenbach

Biesenbach writes about drawing from the word of performance, and he shares his story:

> In the early 2000s, I started a second career as an actor. By day, I served my business clients; by night, I auditioned, rehearsed, and performed. For the longest time, I kept these worlds separate, thinking they had nothing to do with each other. However, the more I studied and performed, the more I realized that the worlds of business and acting were not so different. They both require you to connect with an audience, to express yourself creatively, and, most of all, to tell stories. As I often tell my clients, if you want to stand out and be creative, stop looking at what other businesses are doing and start looking at show business. (pp. 7-8)

In his book *Unleash the Power of Storytelling*, Biesenbach says, "If you want to break down walls with people, truly connect with them, and make an impact, few things beat a well-crafted, well-told story (2018, p.11). He mentions why stories are powerful:

- Great stories cause our palms to sweat, our hearts to race, and our eyes to dilate.
- Emotionally, we empathize with the protagonist; we identify with their struggle.
- Mentally, we put ourselves inside the story, asking the questions, "What would I do in these circumstances? How would I measure up?" (p.13)

In its simplest form, Biesenbach tells us that a story is about a character pursuing a goal in the face of some challenge or obstacle. How the character tries to resolve that challenge drives the narrative. There are undoubtedly other elements to a story—a turning point, climax, finality, and more—but character, goal, and challenge are the three legs of this stool. Without these three, you do not have a story (p. 20).

An example he shares is:

> In the TV classic "I Love Lucy," the character is Lucy Ricardo, the zany redhead living in New York with her bandleader husband. The goal driving much of her action is to get into show business, and her challenges are many: her husband Ricky will not let her in the show, she is not exceptionally talented, and she becomes her own worst enemy throughout her outlandish attempts to win a part. As for the solution, therein lies the legendary 'high jinks' central to this and any sitcom. (p. 21)

Biesenbach's words of wisdom are to always look for stories. The true power of storytelling is to set us apart in a noisy, competitive world.

Robert Garmston

Garmston (2019) states, "Data are a poor instrument for influence" (p. 3). He follows this up with a story about the U.S. Supreme Court hearing a case about political gerrymandering and complaining that the statistical analysis they are receiving is hard to understand. The chief justice called it *sociological gobbledygook.*

Garmston shows us the difference between daytime 'talk' and nighttime 'talk.' He does this through a story about Anthropologist Polly Wiessner, who lived in Namibia among the Ju/'hoansi people when they still existed by hunting and gathering.

She coded conversations involving at least five people. Day talk, she discovered, was quite different from talk at night around a fire. She identified 34% of daytime talk as criticism, complaint, or conflict, including workplace political debates. But the talk was transformed when the sun went down, and the people gathered to reflect on their experiences. Most of the time, people told stories about people they knew, information about earlier generations, and what might be happening in other villages or the spirit world. This kind of talk took 81% of the Ju/'hoansi's communal time (Garmston, 2019, p. 11). Today, 370 million Indigenous people maintain their cultural identity worldwide through stories (p. 12).

Most historians and psychologists believe storytelling is one of the many things that define and bind our humanity. Humans are perhaps the only animals that create and tell stories. In all cultures and ages, storytelling has been the vehicle for human reflection on experience, an ability that separates us from other life forms (Garmston, 2019).

David Herman

Herman tells us that stories can serve as an instrument for distributing intelligence and disseminating knowledge about or ways of engaging with the world across space and time (2013, p. 248). He gives the example that the story reflects and reinforces the individual nature of intelligence—the interconnection between trying to make sense of and being within an environment that extends beyond the self.

A story he shares is about storytellers such as the Beowulf poet, who can extend the focus of concern to situations, participants, and events beyond those about the here-and-now of the moment of the story. That is a means for embedding imagined scenarios within the current context of the talk. Beowulf's poem models how stories provide a context where notes can simultaneously be articulated and promulgated across different communities. In this way, stories make sense of past experiences, map out the course of future events, and assess how assumptions and norms might shape or be shaped by one's own or another's conduct (Herman, 2013, p. 249).

Evelyn Clark

Clark tells us that great leaders know workers need more than lofty mission statements and industry buzzwords. To understand and appreciate what their organization stands for, workers must hear about its people, values, and history. So intelligent leaders tell stories.

Without Stories, What have you got? This was a response from an elderly nursing home resident when asked to define the most important aspect of a successful life. She asked in return, "If at the end of your life, you do not have stories, what have you got?" (Clark, 2004, p. 200)

That same question applies to an organization's life. By defining, refining, and constantly telling its story, an organization clarifies its values, communicates more effectively to its stakeholders, and helps everyone in its circle focus on the vision. Repeatedly telling the story reignites the spark that fuels the organization, draws current stakeholders closer, and attracts new stakeholders who share the organization's values.

Joseph Campbell

What is fascinating about Campbell is his connection of stories to mythology. In an interview with Bill Moyers, Campbell was willing to address the fundamental and challenging subject of myth. A conversation Moyers shares in the book *The Power of Myth (1991)*:

> One of his colleagues asked about the collaboration with Campbell: "Why do you need the mythology? "She held the familiar, modern opinion that "all these Greek gods and stuff' are irrelevant to today's human condition. What she did not know – what most do not know – is that the remnants of all that 'stuff' line the walls of our interior system of belief, like shards of broken pottery in an archaeological site. However, as we are organic beings, there is energy in all that 'stuff,' and rituals evoke it. Consider the position of judges in our society, which Campbell saw in mythological, not sociological, terms. The judge could wear a gray suit to court instead of the magisterial black robe if this position were just a role. The judge's power must be ritualized and mythologized for the law to hold authority beyond mere coercion. (p.xii)

Because I teach college, I find this story delightful:

Campbell gave up pursuing a doctorate and went to the woods to read. He continued to read about the world: anthropology, biology, philosophy, art, history, and religion. He continued to remind others that one sure path into the world runs along the printed page. A few days after Campbell's death, Moyers received a letter from one of Campbell's former students who now helps to edit a major magazine. She wrote:

> "Campbell's 'cyclone of energy blew across all the intellectual possibilities' of the students who sat breathless in his classroom at Sarah Lawrence College. While we all listened spellbound," she wrote, "we did stagger

> under the weight of his weekly reading assignments. Finally, one of the students stood up and confronted him, saying, "I am taking three other courses, you know. All of them assigned reading, you know. How do you expect me to complete all this in a week?" Campbell laughed and said, "I am astonished you tried. You have the rest of your life to do the reading." She concluded, "And I still have not finished – the never-ending example of Campbell's life and work." (p. xiv)

Mastering this art allows stories to transcend time, culture, and even language, turning them into experiences that linger in the minds of listeners and readers. Whether through the written word or spoken performance, the way a story is told—its cadence, tone, and unique voice—ultimately determines its impact. As we conclude this chapter, it is clear that voice is not just an accessory to storytelling; it is the essence that makes a story unforgettable, compelling, and deeply human.

CHAPTER 19

STORYTELLING – FRESH INGREDIENTS

Once upon a time, there was an ancient form of communication called storytelling. It was an essential endeavor. One person talked, and one or more people listened. Then, it fell in disfavor. There are several theories as to why, but most likely, it had something to do with the fact that storytelling did not involve remote controls, fast-forward buttons, joysticks, or social media platforms. The storytelling could have been more flashy. The sound was limited to a person's mouth, with no special effects. Worst of all, you could not brag to your friends about having just spent a month's wages for a state-of-the-art storytelling unit.

Nevertheless, storytelling has enjoyed a resurgence in recent years as people are desperate for human contact or something as basic as looking for storytelling's warmth. Scholars and storytellers reiterate to their audiences that storytelling is more personal than story reading. Many practitioners denoted that storytelling defines cultures, establishes values and standards, and helps people cope with the ever-changing environment. Stories may appear to be simplistic yet are purposeful. However, developmental psychologists point out that stories are not innocent, as they always have a message. These messages have been told over centuries, yet the messages may be lost, unappreciated, and unheard in the clutter of assumptions, caveats, data, and the fear that the storyteller will not be taken seriously.

Lederach (2010) contended that if we intentionally engage each other as humans in relationships, there is dignity and humanity present in the organizations. The story should be something different than a tool or a means to provide information. A story, just like the storyteller, must have integrity; of course, the story can be the stimulus for a discussion that engages the listeners and the storyteller. A Julia Child's culinary dictum as a metaphor would be that one does not need to cook fancy or complicated food – just good food from fresh ingredients.

Think about your organization in a way that each day you have the privilege to be their leader; that day can be magical. I invite you to travel with me to my house in the country; the sun rises over the eastern mountain. Fog settles into its shoulders. The geese are noisy. The sheep bleat. The mare and her foal trot across the field. Each breath of wind, each flurry of light rain, each bit of good news is miraculous. Savor them. You will not be here forever. Moreover, reject simple explanations for not being the storyteller; as leaders, we should try our best to answer many questions that need to be asked, and at best, a few stories the answers might be worth trying.

For a moment, let us bring in science research and look at storytelling from that aspect –to change it up here for fun! Intuitively, people believe stories can grab and hold human minds. Moreover, we want storytelling to impact, be remembered, and change people's attitudes and actions. Therefore, leaders must ask themselves, do the stories about the organization look like classic once-upon-a-time folk or fairytale stories, and if so, are they effective? The simple answer: not at all. Compelling storytelling is as much a way of thinking, approaching, and planning as the formatted layout or the fixed template of a physical thing: the story. Neuroscientist Anthony Damasio posits that brains automatically do storytelling, naturally and implicitly. Unsurprisingly, stories permeate the entire fabric of organizational cultures (Cron, 2012).

Future thinking is to continue to explore how putting ideas from the art and sciences of mind into dialog with the study of storytelling across media can lead to a richly contextualized account of narrative viewed as a target of interpretation. This account has implications for scholarship on stories and works in the cognitive sciences.

Steve Jobs told us that the most powerful person in the world is the storyteller. The storyteller sets an entire generation's vision, values, and agenda. As an organization leader, have you created a story room and asked if anyone on the team needed any help on the team who was building and bringing to life the story you will be telling to your organization? If you still need to create such a room, why not do so?

Authentic storytelling will energize people to action through an inspiring story when working in the worlds of sales, marketing, speaking, and helping to strengthen a brand. As we all should ask, as did Luhn, Pixar storyteller, why are stories so meaningful? Why do stories resonate so effectively with everyone, regardless of age, gender, and culture? When told well, great stories are memorable, impactful, and personal. Old or new, strictly true or wildly made-up, great stories move people. The human race is drawn like magnets to real stories. They intrigue us. They put voice to the things we want and believe in.

CHAPTER 20

PRACTICE BEING A STORYTELLER

Theatre in South Africa is deeply entrenched in the art of storytelling (Batzofin & Muftic, 2022). People live, speak, and move with stories embodied in performance practices called *Antigone* (not quite/quiet).

Why can some people tell great stories while others claim they have none? Since the beginning of humanity, stories have been the communication vehicle that delivers historical events and religious beliefs and builds significant organizations.

Many practitioners indicate that storytelling defines cultures, establishes values and standards, and helps people cope with the ever-changing environment. Messages have been told over centuries, yet they may be lost, unappreciated, and unheard in the clutter of assumptions, caveats, data, and the fear that the storyteller will be seen as a whimsical leader.

Ultimately, storytelling is about the exchange of ideas, about growth – and that is learning. That is why we believe that it is vital that we embed storytelling in our organizational cultures. Storytelling is essential. If you are trying to engage, influence, teach, or inspire others, you should tell or listen to a story and encourage others to tell a story with you. You will have plenty of science to back you up (Peterson, 2017).

Let me introduce you to a book that is fun to read and filled with ideas and practices for harnessing the power of good storytelling and translating data and facts into figures into rich, captivating messages: *Business Storytelling for Dummies*, written by Dietz and Silverman (2014).

In one of my favorite chapters, Dietz and Silverman identify five ways to embed storytelling into the organization's DNA. My favorite of the five is this.

> Propose a small story initiative where leaders and staff learn and try out the skills that move them toward a goal or where they contribute stories to a *story catalog* that everyone can access in their work.

Remember, earlier in this book, we introduced Dr. Trent, who echoes what other authors told us: If the story remains in us, it continues to be painful. Being courageous will help us stop being silent; otherwise, our voices will be buried. Our stories have power because we all embrace our collective vulnerability and worthiness through them.

As the organizational storyteller, you must create an environment for stories to be told. Organizational stories need to be told, as there is a richness in our diversity because we are not monolithic. The beauty of our differences will bring a cross-pollination that will enrich the organizational culture.

Leaders live, speak, draw, and move stories in embodied practices. A storytelling space is the flow and exchange of text transformation into images, text into sound, and movements into emotion. All people use storytelling to preserve their history, traditional culture, and ritual ceremonies (Forest, 2007).

According to Batzofin and Muftic:

> Stories provide us with truth; they take the debris of our lives and give those shards a sense of narrative, form, and verity. The story offers insight but never closer. These traditions are in the care of the storyteller. (2022)

As leaders seek to influence others to create more value for an organization, many have utilized storytelling skills. Influential leaders put words to the formless longings and deeply felt needs of others. They create communities out of words (Paden, 2011). Telling stories inspires action and brings about change in ways that other forms of communication cannot. Stories assist many organizations in better understanding the need for transformation and uniting under one umbrella (Denning, 2005).

We know that storytelling is used as a sensemaking strategy in complex environments. The creative storytelling process and its role in leading are significant talents to use. The talent encompasses choosing the right story for the leadership challenge, storytelling performance, and narrative patterns. Your role is to select those stories that motivate, build trust, and create a vision. Additionally, leaders should be able to use narrative to ignite action, implement new ideas, solve innovation paradoxes, and become interactive leaders (McKinnon, 2006).

Telling a well-crafted story remains a compelling, imaginative experience. A storyteller's intentional and aesthetic choice of story, metaphor, and language can influentially shape and direct a listener's thinking, motive and inspire action, and initiate social change. Stories can be an asset in addressing significant change within organizations if leaders consider utilizing them in the following ways (McKinnon, 2006):

Create the vision: Craft future stories and use illustrated story maps to bring them to life and encourage others to join in. Use metaphors to create a shared team vision, a road map for a new organizational strategy, the future vision for a high-tech merger, and personal stories to convey the essence of a complex issue for a skeptical audience.

Make a positive beginning: Share stories to uncover what the organization is and what it must become, affirming what will not change. Evoke stories to understand what people value.

Step off the edge into the future: Use stories to communicate the need for change and let go of limiting identity perceptions. Tell past success stories as proof that the organization is capable of changing.

Shift resistance and accelerate change: Find stories that turn abstract conceptual ideas into images that clarify purpose, inspire shared meaning, and promote trust and engagement.

Break through to new perceptions: Use stories to promote a new paradigm, open new perceptions about work, and sustain change.

Embrace your humanity: Sharing authentic stories or bringing them to life can do more than strengthen respect and cooperation. It can ignite courage, spark fresh insights, and reaffirm the emotional bonds between employees and the organization.

Demonstrate an understanding of emotional archeology: Involve the emotional states of past societies through material objects and cultural landscapes. Emphasize the need for heart-centered practice.

Stories have the unique ability to humanize challenges, fostering empathy and emotional connections. By framing change relatable and compellingly, leaders can encourage a unified effort toward achieving organizational goals. A well-crafted story is a powerful and imaginative experience that shapes thoughts, inspires action, and drives social change. This transformation highlights the enduring impact of storytelling as a form of artistic expression and a tool for encouraging individuals and communities to think differently and act purposefully.

CHAPTER 21

THAT IS ALL, FOLKS

Ok, I borrowed that from Porky Pig!

Why this book? Questions to ask, according to Herman (2013), are: How do people make sense of stories? Moreover, how do people use stories to make sense of the world? In answering those two questions, thousands of books have been published on leadership, but only a few have hinted at the connection between leadership and storytelling. Thus, with wisdom and a healthy dose of wit, the purpose of this book was to recapture the sense of wonder in storytelling as a practical guide for leaders of today and tomorrow.

Organizational storytelling is like 'feeling free to jump in many puddles' (Gregerman, 2000, p.xiii). Leading by storytelling is not about starting 'in a box to begin with' – it is about constantly exploring new ways of thinking and working, fueled by dramatic changes in leadership. These changes include rapid technological advances, changes in notions about work, the emergence of new markets and new sources of competition, and the impact of new business arrangements such as strategic alliances, changing economics, and demographics (Gregerman, 2000).

We are living through a time of unprecedented and troubling change. We have come to a crossroads where old and familiar customs break down, but the new oral frame and social structure we urgently need is still evolving. We enter the future less connected to ancestral guidance than any human generation before us. Although we have invented remarkable technologies for saving data, we need to remember our organizational stories. We broadcast our voices over vast distances but talk less to those around us. Haunting these changes is the specter of continuing violence, planetary degradation, and the danger that we will come to believe the message that resistance is futile. The old stories teach us that resistance is never futile (Yashinsky, 2004, p.xiv).

When Wade Davis met with an ancient tribal elder, he was told:

> In the first years, you live beneath the shadow of the past. Too young to know what to do. In your last years, you find you are too old to understand the world coming at you from behind. In between is a small and narrow beam of light that illuminates your life. The small, narrow beam of light that illuminates your life can help illuminate so many lives; that is the responsibility and privilege to lead. (Ahmad, 2023)

It is stories that change the world. Not bullet points or bullets. The role of storytelling is about giving hope and helping to present a future, possibilities for a future that can be realized. We, as storytellers, tell stories to inspire people who want to make a world they want to live in.

All stories have a message. What is your message when telling a story? Could it be as simple as:

> A fisherman stops at a fishing store to buy some tackle, the stuff to put on the end of the fishing line to catch the fish. When he walks in, he sees all these different types of tackle, different colors, different shapes, and different sizes.
>
> The fisherman goes to the store owner and says, "Wow, you have so many different colors of fish tackle here. Do the fish really like these different colors?" The store owner looks at the fisherman and says, "Sir, I do not sell to the fish."….

REFERENCES

Aaker, J., & Bagdonas, N. (2021). *Humor, Seriously.* Random House.

Abramo, L. (2017). *Bridging the PM Competency Gap.* J. Ross Publishing.

Adichie, C.N. (2009). *The Danger of a Single Sory.* TED Conference. https://www.youtube.com/watch?v=

Ajaz, A. (2023). *Solving the Leadership Crisis.* Podcast. https://podtail.se/podcast/future-of-storytelling/solving-the-leadership-crisis-ajaz-ahmed/

Angelou, M. (2009). *I know why the caged bird sings.* Ballantine Books.

Armstrong, P. (2020). *Stories and the brain: The Neuroscience of the narrative.* John Hopkins University Press.

Atlee, T. (n/d). The power of story-The story paradigm. https://www.co-intelligence.org/I-powerfstory.html

Bateson, M. (2011). *The leader's guide to storytelling: Mastering the art and the discipline of business narrative.* Josey-Bass.

Batzofin, J., & Muftić, S. (2022). The digital archive as storyteller. *South African Theatre Journal, 35*(3), 227–242

Biesenbach, R. (2018). *Unleash the power of storytelling.* Eastlawn Media.

Blanchard, K., & Bowles, S. (1997). *Gung Ho!* William Morrow.

Boje, D. (2008). *Storytelling Organizations.* Sage.

Boris, V., & Peterson, L. (2018). *Telling stories: How leaders can influence, teach, and inspire.* Havard Business Review Publishing.

Bronstein, D. (2016). *Aristotle on Knowledge and Learning.* Oxford University Press.

Brown, B. (2022). *Atlas of the heart.* Random House.

Brown, B. (2018). *Dare to lead.* Random House.

Brown, P. C., Roediger, H. L. III, & McDaniel, M. A. (2014). *Make it stick: The science of successful learning.* The Belknap Press of Harvard University Press.

Burroughs, W.S. (1962). *The Naked Lunch.* Grove Press.

Campbell, J. (2008). *The hero with a thousand faces.* New World Library.

Campbell, J. (1991). *The power of myth.* Random House.

Cheng, D., & Wang, L. (2014). Examining the energizing effects of humor: The influence of humor on persistence behavior. *Journal of Business and Psychology*, 1-14.

Clark, E. (2004). *Around the corporate campfire.* C&C Publishing.

Chemers, M.M. (2023). *Ghost Light: An introductory handbook for Dramaturgy*, 2nd Ed. Southern Illinois University Press.

Choy, E.K. (2017). *Let the story do the work.* American Management Association.

Cron, L. (2012). *Wired for story.* Ten-Speed Press.

Davis, D. (2014). *How the story transforms the teller.* TEDx Charlottesville. https://youtu.be/wgeh4xhSA2Q?si=fPOqCLxm5psNKsgz

Denning, S. (2004). *Squirrel, Inc.* Jossey-Bass.

Denning, S. (2011). *The leader's guide to storytelling: Mastering the art and discipline of business narrative.* Jossey-Bass.

Depree, M. (2011). *Leadership is an Art.* Doubleday.

Dicks, M. (2018). *Storyworthy: Engage, teach, persuade, and change your life through the power of storytelling.* New World Library.

Dietz, K., & Silverman, L. (2014). *Business storytelling for dummies.* John Wiley & Sons.

Dzurec, L. (2020). Examining 'sticky' storytelling and moral claims as the essence of workplace bullying. *Nursing Outlook, 5*, pp. 647–656.

Eber, K. (2021). *How your brain responds to stories -- and why they are crucial for leaders.* TED. https://youtu.be/uJfGby1C3C4?si=bVEtKOCxYnDit3MJ

Essex, E. M., & Mainemelis, C. Learning from an artist about organizations: The poetry and prose of David Whyte at work. *Journal of Management Inquiry, 11*(2), 148–159.

Farrell, N. (2018). Leo Li becomes Imagination's CEO. https://www.fudzilla.com/news/graphics/45955-leo-li-become-s-imagination-s-chief-executive-officer

Forest, H. (2007). *Inside story: An arts-based exploration of the creative process of storyteller as a leader.* Dissertation, Antioch University.

Frei, F., & Morris, A. (2023). Storytelling that drives bold change. *Harvard Business Review*, 65.

Fulghum, R. (1991). *Uh-Oh.* Villard Books.

Garcia, G., & Garcia A.G. (2016). *Thoughts from the heart.* Xlibris.

Garmston, R. J. (2019). *The astonishing power of storytelling.* Corwin Publishing.

Godin, S. (2009). *The purple cow.* Penguin Books.

Golden, J. (2013). *Those who tell the stories rule the world – Hopi proverb.* https://mygoldenscribe.com/

Gray, D., Brown, S., & Macanufo. J. (2010). *Gamestorming.* O'Reilly Media.

Gregerman, A. (2000). *Lessons from the sandbox.* Contemporary Books.

Hall, K. (2019). *Stories that stick.* Harper Collins.

Hamel, G., & Zanini, M. (2020). *Humanocracy.* Harvard Business Review Press.

Hardiman, M. (2012). *The brain-targeted teaching model.* Sage.

Haven, K. (2007). *Story proof: The science behind the startling power of story.* Libraries Unlimited.

Herman, D. (2013). *Storytelling and the sciences of mind.* MIT Press.

Hutchens, D. (2021). *Story dash.* Matt Holt.

Ibarra, H., & Kent, L. (2005). What's your story? *Harvard Business Review.*

Irving, J. (2022). *The C2 factor for leadership.* Routledge.

Jabr, F. (2019). The story of storytelling. *Harper's Magazine.*

Jones, S. (2017). *The psychology of stories: The storytelling formula our brains crave.* https://blog.hubspot.com/marketing/psychology-of-stories-storytelling-formula.

Kane, A. (1995). *The dreamer awakes.* Broadview Press.

Kelly, E. (2005). *Powerful times: Rising to the challenge of our uncertain world.* Wharton School Publishing.

Kerr, M. (2013). *The humor advantage: Why some businesses are laughing all the way to the bank.* Micheal Kerr Publishing.

Kirsner, N. (2017). *Storytelling, storydoing, and the brain.* Whole Being Institute. Https://wholebeinginstitute.com/storytelling-storydoing-brain/

Lawrence, R.L., & Paige, D.S. (2016). What Our Ancestors Knew: Teaching and Learning through Storytelling. *New Directions for Adult and Continuing Education, 2016*, pp. 63–72.

Lederach, J.P. (2012). *The moral imagination: The art and soul of building peace.* Oxford University Press.

Li, L. (2018). Leo Li becomes Imagination's Chief Executive Officer. https://www.fudzilla.com/news/graphics/45955-leo-li-become-s-imagination-s-chief-executive-officer#:~:text=Imagination%20Technologies%20has%20named%20Dr%20Leo%20Li%20as,after%20the%20company%20has%20lost%20its%20Apple%20contract.

Luhn, M. (2018). *The best story wins.* Morgan James Publishing.

Lwin, S.M. (2010). Capturing the dynamics of narrative development in an oral storytelling performance: A multimodal perspective. *Language and Literature, 19*(4), 357–377.

Martinez-Conde, S., Alexander, R., Blum, D., Britton, N., Lipska, B., Quirk, G., Swiss, J., Willems, R., & Macknik, S. (2019). The storytelling brain: How neuroscience stories help bridge the gap between research and society. *Journal of Neuroscience*, 8285-8290.

McKinnon, N. (2006). We have never done it this way: Prompting organizational change through stories. Jossey-Bass.

Meade, L. (2021). *The power of story: The secret ingredient to making any speech memorable.* Press Books.

Mogharreban, M. (2018). *How leaders tell stories.* TEDx SunValley.

Montague, T. (2013). *True Story: How to combine story and action to transform your business.* Harvard Business Review Press.

Paden, M. (2011). *Storytelling strategies for leading change in university prestige.* Dissertation, Pepperdine Digital Commons.

Peters, T. (1994). *The pursuit of WOW!* Vintage.

Peterson, L. (2017). *The Science behind the art of storytelling.* https://www.harvardbusiness.org/the-science-behinf-the-art-of-storytelling/

Powers, R. (2018). *The overstory.* W.W. Norton & Company.

Reeves, M. & Fuller, J. (2021). *The imagination machine.* Harvard Business Review Press,.

Rukeyser, M. (1968). *The speed of darkness.* Random House.

Rutledge, P. (2011). *Story power: The psychology of story.* http://www.pamelarutledge.com/story-

Simard, S. (2021). *Finding the mother tree.* Alfred A. Knopf.

Smith, J. (2022). *10 Reasons why humor is a key to success at work.* https://www.forbes.com/sites/jacquelynsmith/2013/05/03/10-reasons-why-humor-is-a-key-to-success-at-work/

Simmons, A. (2019). *The Story Factor.* Basic Books.

Susman, S. (2023). Communication and leadership: Not only entwined but inseparable. *Hesselbein & Company, 2023*(11), pp. 25-31.

Stor, W. (2020). *The science of storytelling.* Abrams Press.

Tichy, N. (2007). *The leadership engine: Building leaders at every level.* HarperBusiness Books.

Trent, T. (2017). *The awakened woman.* Simon & Schuster.

Trinkoff, H.P. (2015). *Storytelling in Art Museums.* Seton Hall University, Dissertation.

Vora, S. (2019). *The power of storytelling.* Sage.

Weischenk, S. (2014). Your brain is on stories. https://www.psychologytoday.com/us/blog/brain-wise/201411/your-brain-on-stories

Williams, J.P. (2019). *'Chief Storytellers': The Newest City Trend?* https://www.usnews.com/news/cities/articles/2019-05-14/denver-atlanta-and-detroit-hire-chief-storytellers-to-shape-city-narratives

Woo, E. *Mathematics is the sense you never knew you had,* TEDTalks Australia. https://www.youtube.com/watch?V=PXwStuNw14.

Yashinsky, D. (2004). *Suddenly they heard footsteps: Storytelling for the twenty-first century.* First University Press of Mississippi.

Zak, P.J. (2013). How stories change the brain. *Greater Good Magazine.*

Zak, P. J. (2014). Why your brain loves good storytelling. *Harvard Business Review.*